1. Hand feed your dog. This teaches him to like human hands, even near his food bowl. It also gets him to like getting his kibble as a treat.

Hand feeding is perhaps the most enjoyable and important exercise of all. The dog learns to enjoy people near his food bowl, and he learns "off," "take it," and "gently." The dog also learns "sit," "down," and "stand," and his kibble increases in value as a training tool. The exercise is better if you get family and friends to do this for you. The dog also becomes socialized toward other people and other people train your dog for you.

2. Make a habit of weighing out your dog's kibble in the morning. Put it in a container and use it as training treats throughout the day.

3. Catch your dog in the act of doing something right, such as lying down quietly, and praise him for it and offer a piece of kibble.

The Lazy Way
alpha books

One luxurious
bubble bath

The Lazy Way
alpha books

Access to most comfortable
chair and favorite TV show

The Lazy Way
alpha books

One half-hour massage
(will need to recruit spouse, child, friend)

The Lazy Way
alpha books

Time to recline and listen to a favorite CD
(or at least one song)

cut

4. Whenever you have 10 seconds to spare, call your dog and ask him to sit. Then give him a treat.

5. Whenever you have 30 seconds to spare, call your dog and ask him to settle down beside you. Then give him a treat.

6. Hug your dog. Touching your dog all over (especially while offering treats), including his ears and paws, desensitizes him to being handled. This also will make your veterinarian very happy.

7. When you have company, ask them to hand feed and handle your dog. This teaches him to like people.

8. Specifically invite people to hand feed and lure/reward train your dog for you.

9. Invite children around to feed and train your dog. This teaches your dog to like and respect children.

10. Get your dog fixed on an object like a stuffed chew toy. This will eliminate inappropriate barking and chewing and will teach your dog to settle down. This also is a great distraction if your dog gets weirded out by anyone—just show him his favorite toy!

cut

Train Your Dog

The Lazy Way™

Train Your Dog

Andrea Arden

Macmillan • USA

Dedicated to my mother and our peanut butter sandwiches.

Macmillan Publishing books may be purchased for business or sales promotional use. For information please write: Special Markets Department, Macmillan Publishing USA, 1633 Broadway, New York, NY 10019.

ISBN: 0-87605-180-8

2000 99 8 7 6 5 4 3 2 1

Interpretation of the printing code: the rightmost number of the first series of numbers is the year of the book's printing. For example, a printing code of 99-1 shows that the first printing occurred in 1999.

Printed in the United States of America

Book Design: Madhouse Studios

Photos: Peter Morris

Page creation by Carrie Allen and Heather Pope.

You Don't Have to Feel Guilty Anymore!

IT'S O.K. TO DO IT *THE LAZY WAY!*

It seems every time we turn around, we're given more responsibility, more information to absorb, more places we need to go, and more numbers, dates, and names to remember. Both our bodies and our minds are already on overload. And we know what happens next—cleaning the house, balancing the checkbook, and cooking dinner get put off until "tomorrow" and eventually fall by the wayside.

So let's be frank—we're all starting to feel a bit guilty about the dirty laundry, stacks of ATM slips, and Chinese take-out. Just thinking about tackling those terrible tasks makes you exhausted, right? If only there were an easy, effortless way to get this stuff done! (And done right!)

There is—*The Lazy Way*! By providing the pain-free way to do something—including tons of shortcuts and time-saving tips, as well as lists of all the stuff you'll ever need to get it done efficiently—*The Lazy Way* series cuts through all of the time-wasting thought processes and laborious exercises. You'll discover the secrets of those who have figured out *The Lazy Way*. You'll get things done in half the time it takes the average person—and then will sit back and smugly consider those poor suckers who haven't discovered *The Lazy Way* yet. With *The Lazy Way* you'll learn how to put in minimal effort and get maximum results so you can devote your attention and energy to the pleasures in life!

THE LAZY WAY PROMISE

Everyone on *The Lazy Way* staff promises that, if you adopt *The Lazy Way* philosophy, you'll never break a sweat, you'll barely lift a finger, you won't put strain on your brain, and you'll have plenty of time to put up your feet. We guarantee you will find that these activities are no longer hardships, since you're doing them *The Lazy Way*. We also firmly support taking breaks and encourage rewarding yourself (we even offer our suggestions in each book!). With *The Lazy Way*, the only thing you'll be overwhelmed by is all of your newfound free time!

THE LAZY WAY SPECIAL FEATURES

Every book in our series features the following sidebars in the margins, all designed to save you time and aggravation down the road.

- **"Quick n' Painless"**—shortcuts that get the job done fast.
- **"You'll Thank Yourself Later"**—advice that saves time down the road.
- **"A Complete Waste of Time"**—warnings that spare countless headaches and squandered hours.
- **"If You're So Inclined"**—optional tips for moments of inspired added effort.
- **"The Lazy Way"**—rewards to make the task more pleasurable.

If you've either decided to give up altogether or have taken a strong interest in the subject, you'll find information on hiring outside help with "How to Get Someone Else to Do It" as well as further reading recommendations in "If You Want to Learn More, Read These." In addition, there's an only-what-you-need-to-know glossary of terms and product names ("If You Don't Know What It Means/Does, Look Here") as well as "It's Time for Your Reward"—fun and relaxing ways to treat yourself for a job well done.

With *The Lazy Way* series, you'll find that getting the job done has never been so painless!

Series Editor
Amy Gordon

Editorial Director
Gary Krebs

Director of Creative Services
Michele Laseau

Cover Designer
Michael Freeland

Developmental Editor
Michele Matrisciani

Developmental Editor
Richard A. Thomas, Jr.

Production Editor
Stephanie Mohler

What's in This Book

TRAIN YOUR DOG The Lazy Way

It Doesn't Have to Be a Pain to Train

With today's hectic schedules, lack of time is a fact of life, not something to feel guilty about. Unfortunately, most dog trainers develop methods that require a great deal of time. If you don't have the time to spend, a chore that is not quick and easy won't—*and can't*—be accomplished. This book shows you methods for training your dog that won't leave you barking for more hours in the day.

You may be wondering why I wrote this book—I'm an expert on lazy dog training! When it comes to busy lifestyles and dog training, I am an authority on both. I have two dogs that I love dearly, and I hold three jobs: dog trainer, writer, and television host. I have very little free time to train my dogs in any way that is not truly effortless, using methods that are easy, efficient, effective, and enjoyable. Furthermore, most trainers come up with methods that require consistency and patience. Most people, however, have little patience and have trouble being consistent; a quick and easy way to train requires less of both.

I have found that, although most people don't have time to add anything to their schedules, the lack of time stems from different circumstances—people are lazy in very different ways.

Throughout this book, you will find special advice about how to be a lazy dog trainer.

There is a stigma attached to the word *lazy* that suggests you aren't willing to give something your all. In this book, however, *lazy* means you are giving 110 percent, and you are using your time in an effective manner: to determine how to do something in a way that doesn't take much effort on the part of either the owner/trainer or the dog. Lazy just means you've chosen to do something in a way that comes easily. So, for example, if the owner wants to train the dog to come when called, she can sit in an armchair while she and someone else call the dog back and forth, "Come here and sit for a piece of kibble!" (This is how you can feed the dog his dinner.) The dog's view of this is "This is a piece of cake. Of course I like recalls! Every time I run up to this person and sit in front of her, I train her to give me a treat!" As far as the dog is concerned, putting out the physical effort to run to his owner is nothing; that's what dogs like to do. It's lazy from the dog's viewpoint as well as from the owner's because it doesn't take a lot of time or effort. There should be no guilt about doing something that is this effortless and easy. It really just means you are thinking about the learning process and making it quicker and easier for the dog (and therefore, for yourself).

YOU'LL THANK YOURSELF LATER

Many people feel they don't have time to train a dog. Not realizing that they *don't* have to spend hours upon hours (time that they don't have) to train a dog, they never bother trying to do it. The other part of the training duo, your dog, hasn't been working from 9 to 5 like you. He's probably expending his energy doing a great job of training *you*. So muster up a little bit of your own energy to train your dog . . . before he trains you!

Acknowledgments

In writing this book I have been strongly influenced by English veterinarian and behaviorist, Dr. Ian Dunbar. In fact, there are extremely few compassionate and thinking dog trainers who have not been influenced by Dr. Dunbar's "lure and reward, fun and games, from-the-dog's-point-of-view" training philosophy.

Over 25 years ago, Dr. Dunbar embarked on an ongoing quest to make pet dog training easy, efficient, effective, and, above all, thoroughly enjoyable for dogs and owners alike. Lucky for dogs, Dr. Dunbar's efforts successfully redefined the very nature of dog training worldwide, heralding a veritable host of long overdue, thoroughly exciting, dog-friendly innovations. In short, Ian Dunbar is peerless in his field, having called most of it into existence.

I am sincerely indebted to Ian for his generous and limitless dog-friendly advice and I offer him my heartfelt thanks. I hope that readers of this book and their lucky dogs will feel similarly indebted to Ian and will soon be partying around the world in celebration of the good doggy doctor.

Part 1

The Dainty Doghouse– What You Need and Where to Get It

Are You Too Lazy to Read The Dainty Doghouse—What You Need and Where to Get It?

1 You consider the dogs featured on your favorite television sitcoms to be good guides in helping you decide what kind of dog you want. "Hey, honey, what kind of dog is that? He just answered the telephone!" ☐ yes ☐ no

2 Your idea of preparing for your dog's homecoming is saving a few of the morning newspapers. ☐ yes ☐ no

3 A crate? Where do you suppose I would find one of those? ☐ yes ☐ no

Painless Prepping for Your Pooch

No matter how easy we make it for you, living with a dog is still a huge responsibility. As hard as it is, this book will help make sharing life with your dog as hassle-free and as effortless as possible. Above all, it will show you how life with your dog can be a whole lot of fun for both of you.

We all know how hard it is to squeeze anything into a busy schedule. But, between long hours at work and commitments at home, it is important *not* to become too casual in your commitment to your dog. When you invite a dog to live with you, you become responsible for his physical and emotional well-being and his education.

With dog ownership, as with most things, preparation is the key to success. This chapter details the bare essentials—what you *absolutely* need in order to prepare for the arrival of your dog—and offers suggestions for organizing both your time and your home.

Basically, you need to prepare two things: your house (discussed extensively in Chapter 3, "Prior Preparation Prompts Peak Pup Performance") and yourself.

PREPARING YOURSELF IN A JIFFY

A prerequisite of an uncomplicated dog-training program is establishing priorities. People often waste a lot of time on things that really are not that important. When it comes down to getting a dog, you should focus on:

1. Which dog to bring into your life

2. How you want your dog to behave

3. How you are going to go about teaching your dog to behave

TRACKING DOWN THE RIGHT DOG IS A BREEZE

Though he wouldn't exactly be considered a commodity, your dog is the most essential purchase when it comes to dog training. Finding a dog with a personality compatible with your home and lifestyle is one of the most important ingredients to hassle-free dog training. There are countless important considerations to keep in mind.

Many times, the only thing people really consider when getting a dog is his looks. Although admiring your dog's looks is one of the joys of sharing your life with him, it certainly is not the main ingredient of a successful partnership. Temperament and behavior should be the top priorities.

Learn about a dog's personality and behavior before you bring him home. Knowing what to expect from a dog's temperament before inviting him to live with you will make you a prepared owner—and will make training more easy in the long run!

The Lazy Way

Another important decision is whether to bring a puppy or an adult dog into your home. You also should think about whether you want a mixed breed or a purebred dog. If you decide to go with a purebred, you need to research the breed you want.

TOTALLY TEMPERAMENTAL

When you get right down to it, the most important thing you're looking for in a canine companion is a good temperament. Just like with people, beauty fades but temperament is forever. When selecting a puppy, the only way to get a true idea of her future temperament is to get a good look at her mom, her dad, and as many other relatives as possible. Keep in mind that, for the most part, you will be designing and creating your puppy's temperament as it develops. But, your dog's relatives will give you some idea of what you are starting with.

When choosing an adult dog, however, the name of the game is test driving. Although it certainly is possible to change an adult dog's behavior, it is much more daunting and time consuming than with puppies. Search for a dog with a temperament that is complementary to your own. Look at lots of dogs and spend lots of time interacting with each potential adoptee so you can choose a temperament to your liking.

PRIME-TIME POOCH OR PUPPY LOVE?

The major difference between getting a puppy and getting an adult dog is the total initial time investment required before your new companion reaches good-dog

A COMPLETE WASTE OF TIME

Do not pick your dog by following a fad or by choosing a breed that is popular because it appeared in a major motion picture or a popular TV show. You can always tell which dog breeds appeared frequently on TV or in films the year before by the types of dogs that wind up in shelters.

status. When you get an adult dog, the first two weeks are intensive, but with your help your dog will quickly learn the house rules. Training headway can be made in no time. With a puppy, however, it's a whole different story.

PUPPY LOVE

If you really have your heart set on a puppy, remember that the puppy cuteness factor only carries that little canine so far—and only for 10 weeks at the most. Soon after, it's the "a" word . . . adolescence! During adolescence, your dog is basically an active teenager. When you have to take your dog out every few hours throughout the night, you might find yourself looking lovingly and longingly at your neighbor's faithful old dog that is resting peacefully on the porch next door.

All right, I've tried to help you. I've tried my best to offer good advice. But you want a puppy anyway. Are you a glutton for punishment? Well, I must admit, I too have been a fool for a puppy many times in my life. Don't worry too much, the following section contains some good advice on puppy selection. (Yes, there are even lazy ways to select and train puppies!)

PICKING YOUR NEW PUPPY PAL DOESN'T HAVE TO BE A PAIN!

As with adult dogs, careful selection is important when choosing a puppy. The biggest problem with acquiring a puppy is that far too many people do so on impulse. It is difficult to walk away from an adorable little puppy face when you have convinced yourself that it's saying "Please take me home with you."

A COMPLETE WASTE OF TIME

The following are the three worst reasons to choose a puppy:

1. Her endearing demeanor. (All puppies are endearing.)

2. Her cute looks. (All puppies are cute.)

3. The prestige of the breed or breeder. (Just because she's a winner in the show ring doesn't mean she'll win in your home.)

Before you make any decisions, make sure that your puppy is as far along in her training as possible before she comes into your home. Surely you don't want to have to play catch up before you even start?

By the time you get your puppy (even if she is only 8 weeks old), she already should be well-socialized and quite well-trained. Look for a home in which the puppies have all been whelped and raised indoors with the family. Growing up indoors, environmental socialization is well underway, and all the puppies will be at least somewhat desensitized to most noises and disturbances. In fact, very little can scare home-grown puppies because they already have been exposed to children crying, adults arguing, pots and pans banging, vacuum cleaners vacuuming, and televisions and radios blaring. They also should already have met all sorts of people by the time you come by for a look.

QUICK PAINLESS

Talk to a few friends who have recently raised a puppy or visit a puppy class and talk to a few owners.

PICKING A PRIME-TIME POOCH

The Top Five Things to Do When Choosing Your Dog

1. Read dog books.

2. Watch dog-training videos.

3. Go to puppy/adult dog classes to learn how to train and test drive dogs.

4. Go to humane societies in your area to test drive adult dogs.

5. Take your time.

Have the breeder demonstrate that the puppy's parents and siblings all will come when called, will sit and lay down when requested, and are friendly with people. If you aren't allowed to meet your puppy's family, there is probably a very good reason for it.

Taking the time to carefully choose an adult dog that already has been trained certainly is the most effortless training option. Most of the work already has been done for you by somebody else. With adult dogs, the old saying "What you see is what you get" usually is very accurate.

Although you have to expend some energy to help your new adult dog adjust to your particular lifestyle, the entire procedure is far less taxing than raising a dog from puppyhood. Instead of training your dog intensively for months, simply test extensively for compatibility and then devote a few weeks to helping your new dog adjust to your lifestyle.

Beware of selecting your dog the way many people choose their spouses—on the basis of good looks, hair color, and confirmation. Sure, your dog may look really cute, but the real question is can you live with him?

Successfully integrating a new adult dog into your home almost entirely comes down to making an informed selection. When choosing a dog to bring home, do not only take into account the dog's good qualities and characteristics. It is essential that you determine all the dog's behavior—temperament and training problems as well. If you base a decision only on the good, bringing a dog into your home can become an absolute nightmare. Remember, good behaviors and bad behaviors are equally and firmly entrenched as habits. (A dog possessing either will be quite resistant to change.)

Keep in mind that just about every dog can become a suitable member of a human family, but that different dogs are more suitable for different people. A dog that is a little bit shy or fearful may make a wonderful companion for a quiet person who lives alone and does not have many visitors. On the other hand, a rambunctious fool of a dog may be the perfect pet for a family with rambunctious children.

INVESTIGATE! BLOODHOUNDS NEVER HAD IT THIS EASY

You would be well-advised to find out a number of important things about a dog before you invite him into your home:

1. The first item on the agenda is to determine whether the dog is well socialized—whether he likes people, especially children and strangers. You also need to determine whether he likes you, your family, and your friends.

2. Next you need to find out whether he likes other dogs and other animals. Obviously, this is especially important if you have other pets at home. It just isn't fair to ruin the lives of your existing animal companions by bringing home an asocial or antisocial dog. Remember, the other animals were there first. It is important that the newcomer gets along with them. Surely you don't want to make life a living nightmare for a resident pet when you bring in a new dog. Just think how you would feel if your dog brought home a really obnoxious and belligerent human to live with you!

YOU'LL THANK YOURSELF LATER

An adult dog's temperament is pretty much set, so take lots and lots of time to select the best dog for you. Bring him home on three days approval before eventually giving your heart to him for a lifetime.

3. It also is smart to find out whether the dog soils the house, chews destructively, or barks or digs excessively. Of course, you have to be realistic. All dogs (and all people, for that matter) have at least some behavioral problems. Moreover, behavioral problems are the most common reason for surrendering dogs to shelters or letting dogs roam during the day (when they often are picked up by animal control and then taken to animal shelters). Consequently, if you are looking at shelter dogs, it is safe to assume that most have one kind of behavior problem or another. It's a good idea to find out why the dog is in the shelter. Many behavior problems can be resolved quite quickly; others are harder to eliminate. House-soiling, destructive chewing and digging can be resolved in a matter of days. Owner-absent barking, on the other hand, may take several weeks to control. Pay particular attention to whether your prospective dog barks, how long he barks and whether you can get his attention while he is barking.

4. Another important consideration is the dog's general activity level. Place it somewhere on a scale that ranges from potato-lethargy to wall-bouncing, utterly rambunctious, turbo-charged hyperactivity.

5. Last but not least, determine the extent of the dog's vocabulary. (Does he understand and respond to commands such as stay and sit?) Also assess his level of basic training.

YOU'LL THANK YOURSELF LATER

Choosing the right dog for your lifestyle is the simplest way to make owning a dog a truly lazy and leisurely endeavor. Though it may take time to find the right dog, once you do, it will be much easier to train the fellow in the future.

CRUISING THE SIDEWALK: TEST DRIVING ROVER

The best way to make the right choice is to approach your search for a dog in much the same way as you would go about looking for a new car—test drive a wide variety of prospective candidates. Certainly, looks are important but so are performance and comfort (or compatibility). Before you start your search in earnest, it might be a good idea to perfect your test-driving skills at a dog-training club or with friends' dogs. Practice on as many dogs as possible to improve your skill at reading dog behavior.

Above all, when searching for the perfect adult dog, beware of giving your heart before checking him out thoroughly. Try to put your heart on hold until you have rigorously test driven the dog and made sure he is suitable for your home and your lifestyle.

TEST DRIVING TIPS

1. Spend as much time with the dog as possible to see whether his behavior and activity level change over time. Most dogs act very differently during the first 5 or 10 minutes of any interaction than they will for the rest of their time with you. Some dogs are so eager to play with a person that their exuberance overshadows their normal independence or stand-offishness. Other dogs appear shy on first meeting—but the shyness may mask the dog's true pushy or overbearing nature.

YOU'LL THANK YOURSELF LATER

Practice makes perfect! The same is true when it comes to training skills. Becoming acquainted with training methods by practicing them on friends' dogs or at dog-training clubs will better prepare you for some of the surprises that your dog may spring on you later.

In addition to test driving a dog to determine his good and bad qualities, see what you can teach him and how quickly and easily he learns. An essential aspect of test driving is finding something the dog doesn't yet know and seeing how quickly you can teach it—and how difficult it is to do so. The dog may look adorable, but you still want to make sure he is trainable. See whether you can lure/reward train the dog to come, sit, lie down and roll over. If the sits are a little slow, bring out some treats and try to speed them up. If the dog is blowing off toys and treats and if he isn't interested in you, how the heck are you going to train the dog once you get him home!?

2. In 15 minutes, how much time does the dog spend paying attention to you?

3. Estimate the dog's general activity level. Is he constantly on-the-go or does he eventually chill out and settle down?

4. Does the dog appear to be fearful and/or aggressive?

5. Does the dog look at you? Does he make contact? (You want a dog that likes you!) It is smart to get a realistic picture of whether the dog would rather interact with you or entertain himself by investigating his immediate surroundings.

6. Does the dog listen to you? Can you get his attention? (Call the dog to come when he is otherwise preoccupied.)

7. You need to determine what the dog knows in terms of basic training. Check to see whether the dog will come when called and whether you can get him to follow. See whether the dog shows any recognition of instructions such as sit and down. Make sure to put the dog on-leash and try him out for a few laps around the block.

8. When choosing a dog, don't expect him to be perfect (although it's wonderful if he is!). Realistically, you can expect all dogs to have some problems. Consequently, the most important thing to

determine is how easy it is to communicate with the dog to modify his behavior. Find out how quickly the dog learns. In other words, how easy he is to teach and train.

Keeping in mind that there are hundreds of breeds of dogs to choose from as well as innumerable mixed breeds, your choice can be a wee bit perplexing. No doubt, however, your decision will be strongly affected by other dogs with whom you have previously shared your life. Past experiences with dogs you grew up with and friends' or neighbors' dogs will have a great influence on your current choice. Don't restrict your choice because of your interactions with a few very special individual dogs. Research dog breeds carefully.

Visit your local bookstore and scan a few books about breeds to get more ideas. You also can visit a local dog show or a shelter to check out a few of your favorite breeds and mixes in the flesh. Be cautioned, however, most breed books are written in glowing terms, and most people you meet at a dog show who are involved with a particular breed may be blinded by their love for their breed.

To get a more realistic idea of how your favorite breeds are likely to turn out, it's a great idea to go to a local puppy- or dog-training class to talk to the pet owners and to test drive a number of dogs. Checking dogs out at a class is easier and is much more revealing than reading any book about dog breeds.

IF YOU'RE SO
INCLINED

There are a plethora of dog breeds to choose from, and finding the dog that is a perfect match for you and your lifestyle can be overwhelming. Visiting puppy classes is the best way to discover the true type for you.

YOU'LL THANK YOURSELF LATER

Look for a puppy that has been raised indoors with the family. If the pup was raised in an outdoor kennel, he already is behind in his socialization and training. In a sense, he is developmentally delayed, and you will be playing catch up.

THE FASTEST WAY TO LEARN WHAT TO EXPECT FROM YOUR NEW DOG

Learning what types of problems to expect from your new puppy is probably the single biggest time-saver in canine companionship because it enables you to be prepared for the troubles ahead.

Again, visiting a local puppy-training class will answer all your questions in one fell swoop. You will experience firsthand puppy owners struggling with a number of puppy problems such as puppy biting, boisterous behavior, fearfulness, house-soiling, destructive chewing, and digging. Similarly, you will notice adolescent and adult dog owners struggling with dogs that pull on-leash, jump up, are hyperactive, bark excessively, and are generally rambunctious.

The wonderful thing about the dog owners you meet (especially the children) is that they will tell you the absolute truth. They'll take all the time in the world to explain to you in great detail all their problems—especially, but not limited to, pet problems. Pet owners also will offer a realistic view of which training methods worked well and which methods were useless. Most importantly, though, pet owners will accurately second guess their own predicament and will, almost sadly, tell you what they wish they had done. Perhaps the laments of pet owners is one of the best advertisements for prior and proper preventative preparation. Many pet owners will implore you to heed their advice and avoid their plight.

You will quickly appreciate that puppy and dog problems you may expect from *your* perspective companion are likely to be the same. Believe it or not, unless taught otherwise, pups grow up to act like dogs. It should come as no surprise, therefore, that puppy/dog behavior, temperament, and training problems all are utterly predictable. Thus, they can be easily prevented.

There generally is a lot of time to talk to owners both before and after class. You also might consider asking whether you can test drive some of their puppies and dogs. To learn about dog behavior and training, there is simply no better teaching aid in the whole world than test driving half a dozen or so adult dogs. See whether you can get them to come, sit, lie down, and roll over. Why? Because if you can't do it with these dogs, how on earth are you going to do it with your *own* dog in just a few weeks time?

Even if you intend to get a young puppy, you should test drive at least half a dozen adult dogs of the breed(s) or type(s) in which you are interested. Adult dogs are great educators—they will teach you everything you need to know about their breed or type. Beware of being duped by PCF—the puppy cuteness factor. Though you may be planning to bring home an 8-week-old puppy, remember that she will have the scary brain of an adolescent and will be almost adult-sized within just three months. Once you get your puppy, the clock is running. Be ready to make a grand, positive impact while she is still very young.

YOU'LL THANK YOURSELF LATER

The best way to really learn about what to expect from dog behavior is to gain experience hands-on. By spending time with the breeds in which you are interested, you can get a glimpse of what it might be like to have that type of dog living with you for the next several years.

If you are worried that your puppy will grow up to be a dog with problem behavior, adopt an adult dog that already is trained and well socialized.

The Lazy Way

Checking out puppies, dogs, and problems in a class also offers a wonderful opportunity to investigate different puppy- and dog-training schools for your dog's future education. Remember, your dog is not going to come trained like Lassie. Lassie was played by *several* highly trained dogs. The only way your dog is going to act anything like Lassie is if you train him right. Call the Association of Pet Dog Trainers (1-800-PET-DOGS) to find a class in your area.

The best way to save time when training your dog is to select an adult dog that already has a solid temperament and good manners. Above all, make sure the dog is compatible with your busy lifestyle. Another option is to adopt a puppy that already is well socialized. Either way, making the right choice in the beginning will save a lot of time and energy later.

The following is a list of the best contacts for more doggie-related information:

1. To find a puppy or dog trainer in your area:

    Association of Pet Dog Trainers
    P.O. Box 385
    Davis, CA 95617
    (800) PET-DOGS
    E-mail: apdtbod@aol.com
    Web site: www.apdt.com

2. For puppy-training books and videos:

    Howell Book House
    1633 Broadway
    New York, NY 10019
    (800) 428-5331

James & Kenneth P

2140 Shattuck A

Berkeley, CA

(510) 658-

3. For an

Dc

Uni

(510) 48

4. For educationa   in your area:

Narnia
Sandy Myers
10143 Clow Creek Road
Plainfield, IL 60544
(630) 904-0895
E-mail: NarniaPets@aol.com
Web site: http://users.aol.com/jemyers/narnia/htm

YOU'LL THANK YOURSELF LATER

You'll thank yourself later if you watch a few dog-training classes, listening carefully and religiously to the laments of puppy and adolescent dog owners who are only a few months ahead of you in the dog-training game. Learn from *their* experience. Spending a little time at classes now will save you a lot of time later!

Puppyworks

Kathleen Chin

P.O. Box 954

Benicia, CA 94510

(707) 745-4237

Fax (707) 745-8310

E-mail: events@puppyworks.com

Web site: www.puppyworks.com

Getting Time on Your Side

Did you ever notice that when you're driving somewhere you've never been before it seems to take forever to get there? And doesn't the return trip always seem to take less time? Even though it seems quicker coming than going, it's really the familiarity of the drive that makes it easier. So, it's safe to say, the more you know about what you are doing (or where you are going), the speedier and more fun it seems! Why should it be any different when dog training? Now that you've read Chapter 1, you have the inside scoop on painless prepping for your pooch. You have determined which dog to bring into your life and how you are going to go about teaching him to behave appropriately. The great thing about these tips is that they increase your familiarity with responsible pet ownership, which can take time and effort. What's even better about *The Lazy Way* is that you won't notice the amount of energy you've expended. It's like that drive in the car—quick and painless—and sooner than you know, you'll arrive home in awe of how much easier it was than before—except now you'll have an adorable new puppy to share your life with!

Chapter two

The Trainer's Teeny Toolbox

Now is the time to debunk the myth that you need lots of expensive supplies to train your dog. Requiring a whole wheelbarrow of equipment is not *The Lazy Way,* the quick way, or the easy way. Excessive equipment all too often is a substitute for lack of knowledge, skills, and technique.

READY, SET, GO!

You can start training your dog right now—without any added equipment. All you really need to train a dog is a working brain and a dog. During training, you will be teaching your dog and developing a relationship with him. Since you will not be forcing, coercing, or dominating your dog, you won't need equipment for restraint and punishment. What you will need is equipment that educates the dog. Basically, all you need is the dog, yourself, and just a few extras.

The additional supplies—other than the obvious ones just mentioned—are briefly discussed here and then are covered further in Chapter 3, "Prior Preparation Prompts Peak Pup Performance." Think of this as a checklist of items you absolutely need to make your stress-free training program a success!

THE TOP 10 TOOLS OF THE TRAINING TRADE

1. Your Dog

As discussed in Chapter 1, "Painless Prepping for Your Pooch," your dog is the most important tool for training. Training a dog without a dog is like washing a car without a . . . well, you get the picture!

2. Yourself

Training is a team sport. You and your partner (your dog) will work together until he is properly trained. Without you as his right-hand person, your dog won't be able to make training work.

3. Attitude

A good heart, gentle hands, and a fair measure of enthusiasm all are essential to proper training.

4. A Dog Bed and a Crate

Your dog needs a dog bed for rest and a crate for short-term close confinement. Be sure *not* to leave your dog in the crate for extended periods of time. You wouldn't want to be locked up in close quarters all day, and your dog doesn't want to be either!

IF YOU'RE SO
INCLINED

Most dog food companies will send you free samples, which you can use as treats for training.

If you have never used a dog crate before, it helps to call it by its proper name, "crate," as opposed to "cage," which can summon negative overtones. If your dog is introduced to his crate in a positive way, he invariably will use it as his own room.

Crates can be made of heavy wire, plastic, fiberglass, or wood. Wire is cooler for your training buddy in warm weather. You can find a variety of models in pet shops or in wholesale animal-supply catalogs.

5. Chew Toys

Your dog needs many durable, stuffable hollow chew toys, and sterilized bones.

6. An Ex-Pen or Baby Gate (Long-Term Confinement Area)

As previously discussed, crates should *not* be used for long-term confinement. For this reason, you need an exercise pen (an ex-pen) or a baby gate. An ex-pen is a collapsible wire pen, used to temporarily confine your dog in a safe area.

7. Two Bowls

You need two bowls for your dog. One bowl must always contain clean water. The second bowl should be used for food. Bowls can be made from many different materials including plastic and porcelain.

QUICK n PAINLESS

Save time and energy by supplying your dog with stainless steel food and water bowls—they're the most sanitary and the easiest to clean.

Confused about which food to feed your dog? Ask your veterinarian to recommend a brand.

The Lazy Way

8. Food

Your dog obviously needs to eat. Dry kibble and treats are important—not only to help him maintain a healthy diet, but to be used as rewards.

All dog foods are not created equal. The primary ingredient of some dog food is ground corn, wheat, or rice. Others use chicken, beef, or lamb plus animal by-products as the main ingredient. The food also might include meat meal and additives, preservatives, and vitamin/mineral packets. The ingredients, as well as the percentage of crude protein, crude fat, crude fiber, and moisture, are listed right on the package or on the label. You can learn to decipher this material, but for most people it's hard to know which bag or can to select.

A good bet is to seek out one of the excellent brands manufactured by a reputable company and sold at pet supply stores.

In keeping with the current health-food trend, many new brands have exceptionally pure, wholesome, and all-natural ingredients. You might have to pay a bit more, but it's worth it to feed your friend well. Your doggie deserves the best.

Knowing what should *not* be included in your dog's diet is just as important as knowing what *should* be included. Avoid soy meal, a cheap source of protein that has been linked to some health troubles. Some dogs do not assimilate ground corn well. Look for natural sources of nutrition such as vitamin A and E and avoid foods that contain the preservatives BHA, BHT, ethoxyquin, and chemicals.

9. A Buckle Collar Plus ID Tag

Invest in a sturdy leather or nylon collar for your adult dog. Choose a less expensive collar for a young puppy—he will grow out of it in no time. Your dog—whether puppy or adult—also needs an ID tag so he can be returned to you if he gets lost.

10. A Leash

A good 6-foot leather leash will last for your dog's lifetime.

NO TIME TO RUN TO THE STORE? SHOP AT HOME!

Most pet stores carry just about everything you'll need for your dog. The truly hassle-free way to shop for yourself, however, also is the truly hassle-free way to shop for your dog. Get a cup of tea or coffee, sit in your most comfortable armchair, and start calling a few of the many wholesale pet-supply companies listed here.

Cherrybrook
Route 57
P.O. Box 15
Broadway, NJ 08808
(800) 524-0820
(908) 689-7979
General pet supplies

QUICK PAINLESS

Utilize meal times as training opportunities. Ask your dog to sit for his supper. Handle your dog and hand feed him at the same time. Put his food in a stuffable toy so he can have a bit of fun trying to get the food out.

IF YOU'RE SO INCLINED

If you're in the market for a crate—either buying or selling—try placing an ad on your vet's bulletin board. Crates usually are no longer necessary once the dog is trained or has outgrown his puppy crate. Posting your ad when looking for a used crate or trying to sell a crate you no longer need should get some responses pretty quickly.

Direct Book Service
Dog & Cat Book Catalogue
P.O. Box 2778
Wenatchee, WA 98807-2778
(800) 776-2665
(509) 663-9115
E-mail: dgctbook@cascade.net
Pet books, including rare and hard to find

Doctors Foster & Smith
2253 Air Park Road
P.O. Box 100
Rhinelander, WI 54501-0100
(800) 826-7206
General pet supplies

Doggone Good!
6429 Pelham Court
San Jose, CA 95123
(800) 660-2665
Web site: www.doggone.com

In the Company of Dogs
P.O. Box 7071
Dover, DE 19903
(800) 924-5050
Specialty gift items for dog lovers

J&B Wholesale
5 Raritan Road
Oakland, NJ 07436
(800) 526-0388
Web site: www.JBPet.com
General pet supplies

K9 Cruiser
4640 Desoto Street
San Diego, CA 92109
(800) 592-7847
Device to make taking your pet on bike rides a safe and fun prospect

Max 200
114 Beach Street Building 5
Rockaway, NJ 08766
(800) HIMAX20 (446-2920)
(973) 983-0450
Fax (973) 983-1368

Pet-Pak, Inc.
P.O. Box 982
Edison, NJ 08818-0982
(800) 217-PETS (7387)
(908) 906-9200
Pet first aid kits

RC Steele
1989 Transit Way, Box 910
Brockport, NY 14420-0910
(800) 872-3773
General pet supplies

YOU'LL THANK YOURSELF LATER

Don't hesitate to ask a salesperson for suggestions and advice about doggie products if you are unsure about what you need.

Getting Time on Your Side

Congratulations! By test driving different breeds and talking to other dog owners you've decided which puppy or dog you are going to adopt. Now the time has come to bring your cuddly companion home to meet his new family. Are you ready? Of course you are! Now that you've read Chapter 2, you have the essential tips you'll need to prepare your house and family for your pup's homecoming. You know which pet products and supplies are necessary for your dog and you've researched the different types of dog food on the market. With the Top 10 Tools of the Training Trade you can pick up the supplies you need in a jiffy. You even discovered how to shop at home through wholesale pet-product suppliers. Buying a bone over the telephone!? Definitely *The Lazy Way.*

Faster Than a Speeding Greyhound

Are You Too Lazy to Read Faster Than a Speeding Greyhound?

1 When your dog has to eliminate, you leave the back door open for his convenience. ☐ yes ☐ no

2 The most socialization your dog gets is when he discovers your daughter's stash of dolls. ☐ yes ☐ no

3 You can play connect-the-dots on your living room rug with all of the doggie accidents you find. ☐ yes ☐ no

Chapter three

Prior Preparation Prompts Peak Pup Performance

This chapter discusses cheap and easy ways to organize and prepare your house before you bring your dog home. You will use the materials mentioned in Chapter 2, "The Trainer's Teeny Toolbox."

It is too late to prepare for your dog after he has already entered your home. Delinquent preparation often necessitates forking out lots of money to redecorate your home and to hire a trainer to retrain your dog—definitely not *The Lazy Way*.

If you allow your dog to make mistakes, the precedent is set for many more mistakes to follow. What your dog learns during the first few days in his new home sets the status quo for years to come. As previously mentioned, lack of preparation by owners is the number one reason so many dogs end up in shelters.

Boys will be boys, girls will be girls, and puppies will be puppies! A puppy will break any rule he doesn't know exists. He will do all the normal, natural, and necessary puppy things—chewing, digging, barking, urinating, and defecating. If your home isn't set up properly, he will make so many mistakes that he will be banished to the basement, the garage, or the backyard—and, eventually, to a new home. If your house is prepared properly, however, a new puppy will make no mistakes at all.

GET A GATE AND A CRATE

Setting up long-term and short-term confinement areas is the name of the game when it comes to prepping your house for a new puppy or adult dog. Early confinement prevents your puppy or dog from getting into trouble. Early confinement also goes a long way to ensure that training will be a speedy and trouble-free endeavor.

Your puppy or dog will benefit from two types of confinement areas—one for short-term confinement and another for long-term confinement. Both confinement areas will prevent your dog from making mistakes around the house, and both will help your dog train himself!

Both long- and short-term confinement prompts your puppy or dog to train himself to chew on chew toys, to not bark excessively, and to relax and settle down calmly. Simply give him a stuffed chew toy or white sterilized bone and he will lay down and chew, chew, chew. He can't bark at the same time as he is chewing, so he is

YOU'LL THANK YOURSELF LATER

1. Prepare your home.
2. Prepare your home.
3. Prepare your home.

learning to be quiet. Truly, the most hassle-free way to train your dog is teaching him to train himself!

PICK A LONG-TERM CONFINEMENT AREA: CHOOSE WISELY NOW, SAVE TIME LATER

When deciding on an area in which to confine your dog, it is best to consider an area with impermeable flooring such as a bathroom, a utility room, a kitchen, or an outdoor run. For most apartments and houses, the bathroom offers one of the best choices for a long-term confinement area. Your puppy or dog's long-term confinement area must have a bed, chew toys, and a water bowl in one corner and a doggy toilet (if not yet housetrained) in the opposite corner.

If you plan to be away from your pup for more than an hour, he needs to be left in this long-term confinement area. The last thing you want to do is force him to soil his sleeping area (the crate)—that will make him extremely difficult to housetrain and, consequently, will take up more time than you have to spare!

Long-term confinement also prevents your pup from making mistakes all over the house. Instead, it confines any problems or accidents to the confinement area. (There is no way the puppy's bladder can hold out for much more than an hour or so.) By spending time in this area, your puppy will learn to sleep and play on one side of his room and to eliminate on the other. This method also works for an adult dog that is not housetrained.

QUICK **n** *PAINLESS*

Use the same surface for your puppy's housetraining toilet that you want him to use as a housetrained adult dog. Consider a large litter box with a roll of grass or even a slab of concrete.

KEEPING YOUR DOGGIE COZY IN A SHORT-TERM CONFINEMENT AREA

When you are at home but cannot pay 200-percent attention to your dog, keep him in a short-term close confinement area such as a dog crate or a tie-down (a short, 2-foot leash tied to an eye-hook in the baseboard) with a comfortable bed and a number of chew toys.

Short-term close confinement prevents your dog from making mistakes around the house. It also strongly inhibits elimination so you can conveniently predict when your puppy or dog will want to go. When you release your dog hourly, show him an appropriate spot and grandly reward him for using it. Be sure not to leave your dog in his short-term confinement area for too long, however, especially not until he has developed some bladder- and bowel-muscle control.

Your dog will appreciate having a bed or a blanket to call his own. (That's not to say he can't share your bed when he is trained.) Put this in his crate with the door left open and voilà! You have a cozy doggy den! The dog's crate (with the door closed) also can double as an ideal short-term confinement area.

THE SIMPLE SOLUTION TO HOUSETRAINING TRANSITIONS— DESIGN A DOGGIE TOILET!

If your vet has told you not to take your puppy out until she has had all her shots, housetraining will be a two-step process—training your dog first to use a toilet inside and then to use a toilet outside.

Many people who paper-train their puppies have a hard time getting the dog to eliminate outside. There is a very simple trick to make the transition from inside to outside instantaneous—make the dog's inside toilet closely resemble the eventual outside toilet! If you want your adult dog to eliminate on the street, purchase a thin concrete slab and place it in a large, low-sided box. If you want your dog to go on grass, place a roll of grass in a low-sided box. This literally changes traditional house-training from a two-step process to a one-step process.

STUFFABLE CHEW TOYS—THE SPEEDIEST WAY TO TRAIN!

Stuffable chew toys prevent and solve countless behavior problems. This is one thing you really don't want to skimp on. Not only does your dog need some form of entertainment to pass the time, confinement with a few chew toys is a not-to-be-missed opportunity to help your dog develop his cherished chew-toy habit. I mean, what else is there to chew? Before your puppy or dog comes home, have a few of these waiting for his arrival.

Stuffing Is a Cinch!

Stuff the chew toys with the dog's kibble or treats and your dog will self-train his chew-toy habit. Each week, have a few prestuffed toys ready and waiting in your fridge. You can use a smear of peanut butter, a dollop of cream cheese, a squirt of cheese from a can, a piece of a meaty dog treat, a bit of leftover vegetable or meat from your fridge, your dog's normal kibble . . . the list goes on and on!

QUICK ➡ PAINLESS

Tie a few of your dog's hollow chew toys inside his crate so he must go in there to play with them.

TWO BOWLS AREN'T ALWAYS BETTER THAN ONE

For the first few days (if not weeks) that your new dog or puppy is home, it's a good idea to use just one bowl. Your dog should have access to water but, instead of putting her food in a bowl and just placing it on the ground, there are some things you can do to get a lot more use out of the food.

Weigh out your dog's dry kibble in the morning and store one-third of it in a canine cookie container along with her daily allotment of treats. (The daily calorie intake of food should be controlled so she does not become fat.) Anytime during the day, anyone can take kibble or treats from the cookie jar to use as lures and/or rewards to train the pup.

The other two-thirds can be used at feeding times to have a fun training session. Ask your dog to go through some sit-down-stand sequences for a few pieces of his meal. You also can put some food in a hollow toy. We may not be allowed to play with our food, but who says our dogs shouldn't?

SIMPLE SAFETY: COLLAR AND TAG HIM!

Your dog should always wear a sturdy leather or nylon collar and a clear ID tag, even in the home. If he ever gets loose, it might be the only way he'll be reunited with his family. Make sure your address and phone number on the tag are kept current.

YOU'LL THANK YOURSELF LATER

Make sure you have at least three stuffable chew toys and three white sterilized bones ready for your new dog's arrival home. Toys should be kept in the dog's bed (crate) during initial training at home. Once the dog is house-trained, the dog's toys all can be kept in a basket so the dog always knows where to find one.

GET A LEASH ON THAT DOG!

A good 6-foot leather leash is a worthwhile investment. Keep your dog on a leash until he is housetrained and until you have taught him what is appropriate to play with. This tip is especially important, not only for the safety of your house, but for the safety of your dog. Think of your dog as a toddler. You wouldn't let a 2-year-old child roam around the house unsupervised, would you?

YOU'LL THANK YOURSELF LATER

Grab your dog's collar often (while it's on him). At the same time, praise him and occasionally offer him a food or toy reward for letting you do it. In an emergency, when you need to get a hold of your dog super fast, you'll be very happy you taught your dog to like it when people grab his collar.

Getting Time on Your Side

The verdict is in: Your puppy is adorable. He's soft, cuddly, and simply irresistible. When he chews on your shoes and rolls in the grass, he is the perfect picture of puppydom—until he grows up. Thanks to the guidelines provided in this chapter, you can get a head start on gaining control of your puppy's behavior before he winds up in the doghouse. You've learned to resist the puppy eyes and establish some ground rules for your puppy to follow. Best of all, you now understand how going the extra mile to behavior train your dog at an early age will actually save time in the long run. Plus, terms like "crate," "long- and short-term confinement areas," and "stuffable chew toy" are no longer foreign to you. You've learned how to turn these items into efficient training tools that your puppy will want to use every day. And now that you're a student of *The Lazy Way* you have an edge over other dog owners that won't lead you and your pup to months and months of retraining.

Chapter four

Time-Saving Training Tips

PREVENTION: EASY AS PIE!

I'll say it again, prevention is the name of the game. It's both the number one training shortcut and the number one time-saver. The age-old saying "Prevention is easier than cure" is extremely true for dog training. Why waste time trying to resolve firmly entrenched bad habits when it is so easy to prevent them in the first place?

All dog problems are predictable and preventable. Do yourself a favor and learn what problems to expect from your dog before you bring him home. Learn how to make adequate preparations to prevent him from developing these problems.

Your dog will likely feel the urge to chew, dig, bark, pee, poop, pull on-leash, and jump up. Without proper socialization, he may even become fearful or aggressive. Such behavior problems all require time-consuming detraining—

a daunting prospect that definitely is *not* for people who don't have all the time in the world. Detraining includes projects you don't want to engage in. The only dog trainer who has to bust his butt training is the one who has been blind to prevention. You have to act as a modern dog trainer—the type who is always looking ahead. Nip it in the bud *now* so you don't have to waste time resolving problems in the future.

SWIFT SOCIALIZATION

Socialization means providing the opportunity for your dog to interact with people—and that's simple! Allow your dog to mingle with you and your family members; especially children. A socialized dog is accustomed to activity in a household, which will ultimately result in a less aggressive and less fearful dog.

Although you might be able to live with a dog that barks, digs, or chews inappropriate items, it is hard to live with a dog that doesn't like people—especially if he doesn't like you! Make sure you socialize the dog so he loves all people, including his training partner.

Socialization is the most pressing concern with any dog. Socialization prevents temperament problems. Behavior and training problems are pretty easily cured with a little resolve and a good work ethic, even in adulthood. Temperament problems, however, can be extremely difficult and time consuming to resolve in adult dogs. It takes a long time, for example, to rehabilitate fearful and aggressive adult dogs.

A COMPLETE WASTE OF TIME

Allowing your new dog to get away with problem behavior will instill bad manners in your pet and will require time-consuming detraining.

After you have socialized your canine companion, you can train other people to help you train your people-friendly dog. These types of projects are discussed in Part 3 of this book.

THE TIMELY TRAINING METHOD

You can walk to the moon or go by rocket. Similarly, you can attempt to train your dog using time-consuming, laborious, and unpleasant methods, or you can teach your friend in a flash—the fun and lazy way! It's your choice. Do yourself and your dog a favor and choose your training method wisely.

By and large, you should stay away from correction methods, which are based on the premise that the dog already is misbehaving before you start. Avoid methods that involve pushing and pulling the dog and jerking him here and there. It will take forever to train him that way, and it will take especially long to accomplish off-leash reliability. These methods, based on domination, repetition, and consistency, all are part of the old, boring, and time-consuming way to train your dog.

In addition to the fact that it's time consuming, it's quite plain to see why training your dog the old-fashioned way doesn't make sense. This method focuses on punishing the dog for making mistakes, and there are so many mistakes your dog can make. For example, there are thousands of items in your house that your dog should not chew on. If he makes mistake after mistake after mistake, you will *constantly* be punishing him. Why not just teach your dog what you *want* him to chew?

IF YOU'RE SO INCLINED

One of the best games to play with any dog is fetch. It makes no difference whether you use a tennis ball or a chew toy. (A chew toy with a string on it can be flung pretty far.) Even better, get a really big ball and have a picnic on top of a hill. (At home, you can sit at the top of the stairs.) Your dog will keep bringing this ball back up the hill (or stairs) to you. This is one of the easiest ways to exercise a dog. Of course, you need to make sure you are in a safe area for your dog to be off-leash. This game of fetch creates a toy habit in the dog. When he is left at home with his toys, he will be interested in playing with them.

If you have a puppy, take him to puppy class and teach him to come when you call him from a play session. No other single training exercise makes as big a difference in adult dog behavior than if a puppy can do good off-leash recall in the middle of heavy distractions. Look for a puppy class that lets the puppies play off-leash.

Don't treat your best friend like your worst enemy. Using the old-fashioned method, you're just teaching your dog that training *and* you are both a drag.

At the same time, some state-of-the-art, cutting-edge dog-training techniques are so old that they are new again. Lure/reward dog-training techniques were brought back into popularity by veterinarian, dog trainer, and all-time good guy Dr. Ian Dunbar.

As with all contemporary methods, emphasis is based on rewarding the dog for good behavior rather than waiting for mistakes to happen and feeling obliged to punish the dog. However, the magic of lure/reward training lies in the sheer speed with which many different responses may be taught, using the dog's food and toys as lures. Basically, the notion is that the dog would be only too willing to oblige if only he knew what his owner wanted. Using lures makes it easier for the dog to understand our instructions.

This type of training is the way to go. Training methods should become more time efficient and easier as they evolve—dog training certainly is moving in the right direction.

Educating your dog is not the long, laborious process it used to be for so many years. It is just teaching your dog a different language, *your* language, so you can enjoy your life with each other.

The hallmark of sophisticated, up-to-date, psychological dog-training techniques primarily is that they are easy, efficient, effective, and above all, extremely enjoyable for all concerned—especially for you and your dog.

DOG TRAINING SHOULD BE . . .

Easy

The up-to-date, modern, psychological dog-training method's salient feature is its ease. Everyone should be able to do it—not only you but your family, friends, and even children. Modern methods make it easier for you to teach other people to train your dog *for* you. That's really the trick behind laborless dog training—having other people do all the work!

Efficient

When you're on a tight schedule, it's essential that the training method takes very little time to master. If it is a difficult, lengthy process, no one will bother—not you and *certainly not* your family and friends.

Enjoyable

Why shouldn't training be enjoyable? Your dog's education should be fun! One of the neat things about fun training is that time passes quickly. You don't even realize you're training—what was once a training task quickly becomes a pleasurable pastime that neither dog nor owner will be eager to see end. When using the right methods, it often is difficult for the dog, the trainer, or onlookers to discern whether it's fun-time or training time!

Effective

Last but not least, the training method must be effective. Obviously, the methods have to work. Otherwise, what's the point? If it works, it's all good!

YOU'LL THANK YOURSELF LATER

Be proactive with all problems. Either prevent them or deal with them while you can change them—don't wait for them to become well-established habits. No matter what the problem, the longer it is allowed to go on, the worse it will get.

SIT BACK AND RELAX: TRAINING OTHER PEOPLE TO TRAIN YOUR DOG

The notion of getting other people to train your dog is a vital ingredient of lazy dog training. Employing other people enables you to sit down and take it easy while directing other people to do the work. More importantly, with liberal use of reward-based methods, your dog quickly learns to love other people—your dog gets socialized!

Make training fun for everyone involved by showing people how to teach your dog tricks and how to play training games. The key is to convince people to want to train your dog—to show them that training your dog can be a lot of fun!

Throwing a training party is the quickest way to address three issues at once: your dog's basic training, troubleshooting problems, and best of all, getting visitors to train your dog for you.

This book contains loads of suggestions for training games and parties. Though you might find it hard to believe now, your dog will eventually come up with a few games of his own!

Lazy dog training at its best occurs when you're not even there. Enlist a little help when your dog is left at home alone. Many of your neighbors and friends probably would love to have a dog but can't for one reason or another. These folks usually fall into one of two age groups: the young and the elderly. You can invite these people to come into your home, watch TV, eat a little from your fridge, and spend some valuable time with

IF YOU'RE SO INCLINED

By throwing a training party you can socialize and train your dog at the same time while enjoying the company of your family and friends.

your dog. This is especially helpful and, with young puppies, it's almost essential. So go out and enlist some volunteer dogsitters.

HANDS-OFF! TRAINING YOUR DOG TO TRAIN HIMSELF

Don't get too excited, this still takes a bit of effort on your part. Some things are so easy to teach your dog, however, that you can just set up the training situation and leave the room. Welcome to the ultra-easy, hassle-free concept of autoshaping, or doggie self-training.

I know it sounds hard to swallow right now, but you'll be absolutely amazed at how simple and effective it is to get your dog to train himself. He'll be trained to chew only on chew toys, to stop incessant barking, to sit when greeting people, and to settle down quietly and calmly when requested. With just a minimal amount of effort, you can set up your home to efficiently autoshape your dog.

PUT YOUR FEET UP: TRAINING FROM YOUR ARMCHAIR

It takes no more than 10 minutes for you to see the miracle of armchair dog training materialize before your very eyes. Sit in an armchair for 10 minutes and watch your dog go through his repertoire. When he does anything you like, give him a treat. You don't even have to say a word. You just need to watch his natural actions and reward him for doing what comes naturally.

QUICK n' PAINLESS

If your dog barks for your attention, sit in a chair and say nothing to him or leave the room. After a few repetitions, he will realize that you do not respond to his barking. Consequently, he will stop.

If you give him a little treat each time he sits on his own, he will quickly figure out that he can train you to give a treat by sitting! Once your dog is sitting happy, you can just approach him and say "Sit." He's going to do it because you've been playing the sit game with him for a day or so. He will associate the treat with the behavior. This time, however, you are going to teach him that, not only does your approach mean to sit, so does saying "Sit."

In short:

1. When he sits, give him a treat.

2. In no time at all, you will have a sit-happy dog. He will have learned that sitting is the best ploy to work you for food treats.

3. If you invite friends over and have them do this same thing, your dog will be trained to like sitting, especially when people are around! During armchair training, you are just convincing your dog that he is training you. Eventually, you can tack the word "Sit" on so he learns to sit on command!

List everything you like to do at home (such as read books, watch TV, work on your computer, and so on). You can train your dog while doing any of these things. Integrate training into your leisure time. In no time, you will learn to train your dog as effectively and effortlessly as possible.

THE WORST TRAINING ADVICE (OR THE BEST WAY TO WASTE YOUR TIME)

Just as people can offer you some great advice, there's also a lot of bad advice floating around. The following are some common examples of bad training advice.

A Bit of Bad Advice #1: You have to dominate your dog to gain his respect.

This incorrect statement is based on an "alpha dog" view of the dog social structure. Dogs do, in fact, choose an alpha, or leader, of their pack. Dogs do have a hierarchy, but it is a harmonious, working hierarchy based on the developmental acceptance of rank. You will not see an adult dog dominating a puppy though brute force. Rather, there is a social balance that relies on communication between the dogs in a pack. Like the pack, you can develop a relationship that thrives on communication and understanding without physically dominating your dog. Your dog will be happy living with you, and you will be happy living with him.

A Bit of Bad Advice #2: Don't use food to train your dog.

Without a doubt, food is the most easy, efficient, effective, and enjoyable way to train your dog. You can use it to lure and to reward, and you can even use it as a bribe occasionally! We want our dogs to do what we request, but that doesn't mean food has to be eliminated from your trainer's toolbox. It just means you should use food

A COMPLETE WASTE OF TIME

Using force or domination to make your dog do what you want will not make him better-behaved, just an intimidated and mistrustful pet.

intelligently to motivate your dog to learn ESL (English as a Second Language).

A Bit of Bad Advice #3: Don't train your dog until he is 6 months old or he will grow out of what you have trained him.

This is just plain nonsense. If he does something as a puppy, he will do it 10-fold as an adult.

QUICK TIPS: THE FAST TRACK TO A SUPERBLY TRAINED DOG

Whenever you have a moment or two to spare, you can run through any of these quick tips that will help you train your dog in no time!

1. Hand feed your dog. This teaches him to like human hands, even near his food bowl. It also gets him to like getting his kibble as a treat.

2. Make a habit of weighing out your dog's kibble in the morning. Put it in a container and use it as training treats throughout the day.

3. Catch your dog in the act of doing something right, such as lying down quietly, and praise him for it and offer a piece of kibble.

4. Whenever you have 10 seconds to spare, call your dog and ask him to sit. Then give him a treat.

5. Whenever you have 30 seconds to spare, call your dog and ask him to settle down beside you. Then give him a treat.

QUICK ⬤ *PAINLESS*

Training your puppy within the first three months of his life will help him develop into a well-adjusted, social dog.

6. Hug your dog. Touching your dog all over (especially while offering treats), including his ears and paws, desensitizes him to being handled. This also will make your veterinarian very happy.

7. When you have company, ask them to hand feed and handle your dog. This teaches him to like people.

8. Specifically invite people to hand feed and lure/reward train your dog for you.

9. Invite children around to feed and train your dog. This teaches your dog to like and respect children.

10. Get your dog fixed on an object like a stuffed chew toy. This will eliminate inappropriate barking and chewing and will teach your dog to settle down. This also is a great distracter if your dog gets weirded out by anyone—just show him his favorite toy!

YOU'LL THANK YOURSELF LATER

Confining a dog with a stuffed chew toy also is a brilliant method for quieting bark-happy dogs. Right from the outset, it teaches them to become recreational *chewers* rather than recreational *barkers*. Certainly, the dog will still bark when the doorbell rings, but he won't engage in the mindless day-long barking that some dogs are forced into because they are so bored.

Getting Time on Your Side

You've succeeded in giving your puppy or dog the foundation he needed to be a good boy. Now the time's come to take it one step further and begin training your dog basic commands. Chapter 4 has taught you that dog training *The Lazy Way* is easy, efficient, enjoyable, and effective. You have probably begun to explore different training options, such as training other people to train your dog and training from your armchair. (Hey, you earned it!) Most important, you were able to learn to speedily and effortlessly train your dog to train himself to chew only on chew toys, to stop incessant barking, to sit when greeting people, and to settle down quickly and calmly when requested. So go ahead and reward yourself for a job well done by showing off your pooch. It's up to you to prove to the world that even busy people can raise a happy, well-trained dog.

Carefree Ways to Curb Your Canine (The Scoop on Cleanup)

This chapter contains some stress-free ways to keep your dog and his surroundings clean. There are even some suggestions for how to teach your dog to clean up after himself!

AVOIDING CLEANUP DUTY

Most people think of ways to properly clean up after dogs, but why not clean up *before* your dog? If an adult dog, during the first couple weeks in his new home (or the first few months for a puppy or an adolescent dog), is living in an area with no clutter and if he just has his stuffed toys out, you pretty much are going to create a problem-free dog. If you leave things lying around (such as socks and toys and newspapers), however, the dog obviously is going to trash the contents of your house. Once again, you have a situation in which proper preparation avoids future aggravation.

This same idea that applies to preventing house cleanup also applies to cleaning up elimination accidents in your house. The real key is to arrange things so you will never have to clean up accidents at all. You need to make sure that, right from the beginning, the dog is developing good habits—specifically the desire or preference to use his little doggie toilet. That is the area that smells most natural to the dog. It is where he will feel most comfortable eliminating because it is where he habitually does so. This also is the place where he can cash in his urine and feces for liver treats, so make sure you reward him for the right behavior.

Confinement is another main aspect of prevention. If you don't let an unhousetrained dog have the run of the house, there is no need to clean up after him. Access to carpeted areas should be especially restricted until your dog is housetrained. It is much harder to clean carpet than linoleum—a simple but often forgotten fact. Keep in mind that a conscientious confinement routine during your dog's first few weeks in his new home will probably allow him total freedom and free-run of the house for years to come.

NO NEED TO BE A NEAT FREAK AFTER ALL!

As for cleaning your dog's toilet, believe it or not, you actually *don't* want to completely eliminate the scent of a dog's urine from this area. The pheromones in dog urine scream to the dog, "This is a dog toilet, urinate here!" While your dog is still building the habit of going in a designated spot, don't worry about scouring the place each day. Realistically, there isn't much you can do to get rid of the scent from your dog's perspective anyway. His sense of smell is so keen that he will be able to detect urine no matter what you use. You really only need to clean the area so human noses aren't offended.

Feces, on the other hand, should be cleaned up immediately for a number of reasons. First, you don't want your dog to become a feces eater. Second, although dogs almost always urinate in the same spot over and over, they usually avoid defecating in areas where feces are already present. If you want your dog to regularly use his doggie toilet to defecate, make sure to clean up the feces regularly. Otherwise, your dog will use other, less appropriate areas. Third, clean up feces for sanitary purposes. (I know, this is an obvious one.)

OOPS! YOUR DOG WAS IN THE WRONG SPOT AT THE RIGHT TIME?

It happens to the best of us. We do our best to make sure that our DIHT (dog in house training) is taken to the doggie toilet often, but prevention isn't fool-proof. When he is not in one of his two confinement areas, we have the dog right by our side so we can keep an eye on him. But then it happens: You're walking through the living room and what do you see? A little present left by your pup. Analyze the situation to see who made the mistake—it wasn't your dog's fault. (All he did was answer nature's call.) Nobody is willing to let the cat out of the bag about who let the pup out of the confinement area, but you have your suspicions. Regardless of who's to blame, it is time to remedy the situation as best you can.

YOU'LL THANK YOURSELF LATER

Groom your dog regularly. Getting your dog used to being groomed or even vacuumed (some dogs love it) is one of the best ways to prevent dog hair from covering your house.

Clean up and dispose of the mess immediately. Accidents should be cleaned up using copious quantities of soap and water. But again, you really are only cleaning up for human noses. Your dog will always know the smell is there. This little accident (due to human error) should be a warning to everyone in the house to be even more diligent about making sure your dog isn't in the wrong place at the right time.

At this point you might be thinking, "Well, what about the dog? Don't I need to let him know that he went in the wrong spot?" The answer is simple—no. There is no point in taking your dog back to the scene of the crime.

If you punish your dog for eliminating in the wrong spot, he learns two things—first, that he doesn't like you as much as he thought (because you will scare him), and second, that you don't like to see him eliminate. If he is a smart little guy, the next time he needs to go to the bathroom, he will be sure to find a spot where you can't see him (such as behind the couch). He will make a point not to eliminate when you take him for a walk. After all, you taught him that you don't like to see that sort of thing.

Dogs are not good generalizers—when they learn something, they tend to learn it very specifically. When you correct him for eliminating in the wrong spot, you are only telling him that you don't want him to use *that particular* spot as his doggie toilet. Think of the thousands of other spots in your home that your dog might think are appropriate.

For these reasons, it is much better—and so important—to make your best effort to ensure that your dog is in the right place (his doggie toilet) at the right time (when he needs to eliminate).

It's pretty easy to tell when your dog needs to go to the bathroom. He usually needs to go just after waking up and playing and about half an hour to an hour after eating or drinking. For puppies under 4 months old, it also is a good rule of thumb to take them to their doggie toilets every hour. Obviously, as a dog matures, he builds better bladder- and bowel-muscle control, so he won't need to be walked as often.

HE MADE THE MESS IN THE FIRST PLACE! TRAINING YOUR DOG TO CLEAN UP FOR HIMSELF

Dogs are like children—they want to play with every toy in succession and to leave them all strewn about the house. It is both easy and fun to train your dog to pick up his toys and to deposit them all into his toy basket. Start with a simple retrieve. The dog will bring you a toy (any toy), and in exchange, you will give him a piece of kibble. Hold one hand under his mouth (for him to drop the toy into it) as you waggle a bit of food in front of his nose and ask him to give you the toy. Hold your hand over the dog's toy basket and, as the dog drops the toy, move your hand. When it hits the basket, give him a treat. Move the basket to the floor and do the same thing. This takes very little time to teach and is lots of fun. Your dog will really enjoy it, and it will save you loads of cleanup time!

YOU'LL THANK YOURSELF LATER

Train your dog to defecate near the place where you dispose of the feces. In the yard, it would be near his doggie trash can; on the street, it would be as near to your front door (and your own cleanup facilities) as possible, or near a public trash can.

Getting Time on Your Side

When it comes to tidying up after your pup, even Mr. Clean can't come to the rescue. But thanks to the scoop on cleanup in this chapter, you know that the quickest way to keep your dog away from your stuff is to keep your stuff away from him. You're able to keep track of the toys, the newspapers, and all of those socks—even housetraining your pup has gotten easier. You're through with wasting time scrubbing your dog's messes out of the carpet because you taught him where to go. And when you're dog isn't quite on target, *The Lazy Way* is here to show you how to deal with your dog when he has an accident. Now you don't have to have your nose rubbed in it to learn how to clean up the quick and hassle-free way!

Part 3

Bet You Never Knew Training Was So Doggone Easy!

Are You Too Lazy to Read Bet You Never Knew Training Was So Doggone Easy?

1 You've actually convinced yourself that the holes your dog chewed through your shoes are in vogue. ☐ yes ☐ no

2 You could swear you read somewhere that the sound of barking dogs has soothing, therapeutic effects on humans. ☐ yes ☐ no

3 Walking has never been so easy since you stopped putting one foot in front of the other. You just rely on your dog to pull you up and down the street. ☐ yes ☐ no

Painless Puppy Training

Raising a new puppy is an entire subject unto itself. Anyone who embarks on this journey should make sure he or she knows exactly what to expect and what to do before-hand.

EXPRESS CHECKOUT: CHECKING OUT THE FACTS

The best way to do this is to attend lots of puppy parties and lots of puppy- and dog-training classes. (Check with your veterinarian, a local training club or school, and the Association of Pet Dog Trainers.) There is no better way to educate yourself on how to educate your dog than to watch what is going on at these events and to talk to other new puppy owners. You can find out what problems can be expected before you bring home your new little bundle of joy.

Prospective new puppy owners also should read the best books and watch the best videos about puppy training. (See the "Still Begging for More?" section at the end of this book for suggestions.)

SHOPPING AROUND WAS NEVER SO MUCH FUN!

Your mission, should you choose to accept it, is to find a puppy that has been raised indoors and that will be very well socialized by the time you pick him up. This should be your top priority; it should far exceed concerns about show records and so on. This puppy's future is going to be all about hanging out with you, your family, and your friends. The sooner he starts down the socialization road- way the better!

This means you should look for a household in which the puppy's socialization and training are already well underway by the time you pick him up. Ask the breeder lots of questions about how this little guy spent the first eight weeks of his life. Most importantly, you want to check that the puppy has been raised indoors with lots of contact with the family. There should be no sounds or actions to which your prospective puppy isn't accus- tomed (within reason, of course). He should be used to loud noises and people talking loudly, especially children.

If you are adopting a puppy from a shelter, try to find one for which the staff and volunteers have done all they can to make sure the puppy has had lots of positive human contact during his stay.

If you know how to raise a puppy, you want to bring him home when he is around 8 weeks old. If you do not know how to raise a puppy and you still want to main- tain full lazy-dog-trainer status, you don't want to bring a dog home until he is at least 2 years old—you want an adult. If this applies to you, this chapter isn't the one you need. The next chapter covers training a new adult.

It also is important to check out the puppy's house-training, chew-toy training, and basic manners. Education should be forging ahead, even though the young pup is only 8 weeks old. If it's not, you and your dog will be in remedial training for a long, long time.

At this stage in his life, the pup should have a pretty good idea how to use a doggie toilet. This does not mean he will be fully housetrained. What has the breeder or prior owner done to make sure your pup comes along with his housetraining? If the answer is nothing, it would take a lot to convince me to take the puppy (and it should take a lot to convince you).

If the pup has been living in a kennel and has been forced to urinate and defecate in his own bedroom, you are going to have a decidedly non-lazy housetraining challenge. You want to get a puppy that has been raised indoors and has already started paper training or that has been taken outside to pee and poop.

Know the person from whom you're getting your dog. Is training underway? (You're not looking for anything fancy, just the rudiments.) Does the pup follow the owner around the room? Can the owner get the puppies to come, sit, lie down, and roll over using a lure? If the pups are not up to scratch, the present owners don't have either the time, the inclination, or the know-how for education. If the dog is not already at this point, it might be a good idea to look elsewhere.

If you plan to get a dog from a breeder, chances are pretty good that your pup will be introduced to lots of people and (more important) to the doggy toilet before you bring him home!

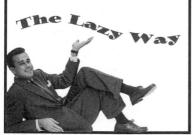

The Lazy Way

Remember, there are lots of puppies around, always remember you are in the driver's seat. You certainly don't want to land one that already is well behind in his education. The present owners will be rid of their puppies within a few days or weeks, but this puppy is going to share your life with you for years. If you truly want to lead a luxuriously lazy life with your puppy, make sure you choose one that already knows what's what.

Don't get bullied by owners who tell you to come and get an untrained puppy that's only 3 months old. A good response to a bully of this kind might be "What do you mean 3 months old and still living in a cage and not even housetrained and doesn't know how to sit and lie down!?!?" This is the puppy you are going to live with. If you truly want to spend time with your puppy that won't complicate your already hectic schedule, make sure he has a good education and knows *how* to live with you. Education should be well under way by 8 weeks old.

PRIOR PUPPY PREPARATION PREVENTS POOR PUPPY PERFORMANCE

Make life easier for yourself—prepare for your puppy. If you know what you're getting into before you get into it, both you and your new pup will glide leisurely through puppyhood and adolescence.

You've got to know how a puppy works. Basically, if you know what to expect from your new puppy and you know how to deal with all the predictable problems that will pop up, preventing these problems becomes easy.

YOU'LL THANK YOURSELF LATER

Knowing how to choose a puppy will set you on the road to manageable, magical puppydom. Go to a pre-puppy party at your local training club and take the time to carefully check out the pup's first home and family.

The most important thing to realize is that, beginning the minute you purchase your new puppy, the clock is running. For every second that goes by while a puppy is living with an uneducated owner in a home that is not prepared, the puppy is developing another habit—and it won't be a good one. You'll have to deal with a two-step process: detraining the bad habits and training the good ones.

This all can be avoided, of course, if your puppy is taught good habits from the outset. It is much easier to just set up the house and the puppy's daily schedule as discussed at the beginning of the book. Basically, the puppy can train himself to learn good habits from the moment he steps his little paws in his new home.

A COMPLETE WASTE OF TIME

Bringing home your dog before you've prepared your home and without a plan of action will create a rocky relationship between you and your dog.

PAINLESS PREPARATION AND A SIMPLE SCHEDULE

The puppy actually should be the third new item to come into the home. The first should be a house preparation plan; the second should be a daily schedule. Most owners make the mistake of working the other way around. They first get the puppy and then two weeks later realize they haven't slept a night, the puppy's out of control, and the house is beginning to get wrecked! All they wind up doing is repair work. This is the type of situation you would like to avoid. Again, prior preparation would have prevented these problems.

Fear not, this chapter provides an easy-to-follow agenda for painless puppyhood preparation.

YOU'LL THANK YOURSELF LATER

One very smart thing to do before you get a puppy is list your priorities. (What is important for you to do? What important lessons do you need to teach this puppy?) Reading this book will help you out, as will watching videos and puppy classes.

WHAT CAN YOU EXPECT FROM YOUR PUPPY?

What can you expect from your pup? Surprise, surprise, he will act like a dog! He will want to investigate the environment with his paws and jaws (he chews); he also will want to destroy objects, urinate, and bark. These actions are as normal as burying a bone and wagging a tail. The puppy also will bite. In fact, he will be a little biting machine.

DEAL NOW, WORRY NOT LATER: LEARN HOW TO HANDLE PROBLEMS BEFORE THEY OCCUR

With preparation in mind, you should know how to deal with problems before you are besieged by them. The following are examples of things you need to know all about:

- How to prepare your house
- How to teach your puppy to tolerate time alone
- How to housetrain your puppy
- How to chew-toy train your puppy
- How to teach your puppy to settle down when requested
- How to socialize your puppy
- How to teach your puppy to mouth gently and, eventually, not at all
- How to teach your puppy when to bark
- How to teach your puppy to shush

- How to teach your puppy to greet people without jumping up
- How to teach other people to teach your dog

THE NAME OF THE GAME IS CONFINEMENT

In terms of preventing problems—which is so much easier, effective, efficient, and enjoyable than solving existing problems—confinement is the name of the game. It is the best way to keep the puppy out of trouble.

When you cannot be with your puppy to direct the proceedings and to train him, keep him confined. When you are home, keep him by your side or in his short-term or long-term confinement area.

When You Are Away from Home

When you're not around, keep your puppy confined in a long-term confinement area that has a comfortable bed, water, lots of toys to play with, and a toilet. Don't choose an area with carpeting (in case of an accident) and consider temporarily covering the floor with a roll of inexpensive plastic flooring (just until the pup is house-trained).

The best long-term confinement area probably is the bathroom. Remove the toilet paper, the towels, the bath mats, and so on. Put a bed in one corner and a toilet in the other. This may sound complicated, but it really only takes a few minutes.

Make sure the toilet is as similar as possible to the eventual intended substrate. If you live in a big city, put

A COMPLETE WASTE OF TIME

There is nothing worse than picking up a new puppy on impulse. It may seem quick n' painless at the time, but it will only make life very difficult later.

down a paving slab. If you want your puppy to eventually eliminate on the grass when he grows up, put down a couple rolls of turf.

It is important to provide the puppy with some form of occupational therapy. Obviously, the puppy can not read this book or do crosswords to amuse himself. He needs to do puppy things. That means chewing on stuff. Make sure there is nothing in the long-term confinement area except chew toys stuffed with treats.

When You Are at Home

When you are at home but cannot pay attention to the dog, put your puppy in a short-term confinement area. A dog crate with a bed inside is ideal. Another alternative is to keep your puppy on a tie-down—a 2- to 3-foot leash tied either to your belt (the umbilical cord method) or to an eye-hook in the wall. You also can tie three or four stuffed chew toys to the same eye hook so they won't roll away from the dog. Your dog must learn to settle down quietly. If you establish the status quo during the first few weeks the puppy is home, there will be no need at all for confinement when he grows up to be an adolescent and then an adult dog. He'll have full run of the house and garden. He will be free for the rest of his lazy life living in your home!

If you let the puppy run all over the place, he will get into lots of mischief—possibly dangerous mischief but certainly mischief. This will annoy you. He will no longer have run of the house because you won't be able to trust him. Instead, he'll be relegated to the yard and will learn

Training a dog to settle down is a snap. Just give him a stuffed chew toy and wait for magic. For serious occupational therapy, you might want to feed him with all his kibble stuffed into half a dozen or so toys. This will keep him calm for hours on end.

The Lazy Way

to dig and bark, causing the neighbors to complain. The puppy's last stop will be your basement or garage (which he will totally wreck with indiscriminate—albeit uneducated—chewing, digging, and house-soiling). Eventually, sadly, your puppy will be forced to leave your home and maybe go to a shelter where he will play the lotto of life.

If you use lots and lots of confinement and lots and lots of rules during the first few weeks your puppy is home, he will surely earn free run of your home for the rest of his happy life.

YOU'LL THANK YOURSELF LATER

Prevent your dog from choking or getting sick by removing all toxic plants, cleaning products, and potentially harmful children's toys from your dog's reach.

AVOID WASTING TIME LATER ON— PUPPY-PROOF YOUR HOME NOW!

The second main consideration when preparing your house is to puppy-proof any rooms to which your puppy may have access. Even though you will be supervising him whenever he is out of his confinement area, you still should remove dangerous items such as toxic plants, small children's toys he could easily swallow, and any toxic cleaning products.

PUPPY'S FIRST FEW WEEKS AT HOME

There is a pretty big agenda during the first week the puppy is home. You have to get his housetraining, chew-toy training, and home-alone training all nailed within the first week. These are three utterly important things to teach. (Each is discussed separately later in the chapter.)

If the puppy is making housetraining and chewing mistakes, is always the center of attention, and never

settles down in the first three days, the precedent has been set for the weeks and months to come. The puppy is going to be a difficult one to train. You will need more than this book and a whole lot more time than you have.

Make sure you set up your puppy's living area and classroom activities so he learns *where* you want him to pee and poop, *what* you want him to chew on, and *when* you want him to settle down quietly.

HOME ALONE

With a new puppy, the number one item on the agenda is to teach him to enjoy life at home alone. This sounds like an unfeeling thing to say, but it also is a sad realization of modern puppydom. In most households, the kids are at school and the adults (or adult) are working. Your puppy must learn to settle down calmly when you are there; that way, he can learn to settle down when you aren't. Try not to smother your puppy with attention during the first few days he is home. Smothering sets a precedent you cannot possibly live up to. You're leading the pup to think he can get attention and affection *ad libitum*. Then, of course, Monday rolls around, no one is home, and the poor pup is all alone. This will make him scared and anxious, and that just isn't fair. This poor puppy, which is a social animal, has been invited into your home but is going to be left there alone for 8 to 10 hours a day.

Individual owners must decide for themselves whether they think this setup is entirely fair. Regardless, if your puppy will be left at home alone, you had better teach him how to enjoy passing the time of day.

Your puppy needs to learn what types of occupational therapy are considered appropriate in a human dwelling. Otherwise, he will happily improvise during his quest for hobbies—barking, chewing, digging, house-soiling . . . Soon you won't have a dwelling to dwell in—get the picture?

The best thing to do here, of course, is to start training the puppy when you are home. Don't let the puppy have unlimited contact with you when you're there because he will miss you even more when you are gone. Instead, when you are home, let the puppy have some quiet moments in his crate with, of course, some stuffed chew toys. Toys work brilliantly. As the puppy chews on the chew toys, he teaches himself many things. And all this time, he will be settled down.

Start early. Remember, preventing is easier and quicker than curing, and good habits are just as difficult to break as bad ones. Be sure to establish good habits from the beginning. Only after you have taught your pup to enjoy your absence with stress-free independence and confidence should you smother him with affection when you are at home.

HASSLE-FREE HOUSETRAINING

After you have made sure the house is set up, you can see to it that your puppy has grasped the idea of where you want him to pee and poop. This means you will have chosen long-term and short-term confinement areas before your dog comes into the home. You also should sit down with everyone in the household and go over the puppy's

QUICK ⬤ PAINLESS

If you sometimes can't give your dog the attention he deserves, throw him a stuffed chew toy. Most likely your dog will discover that playing with chew toys is much more interesting than hanging around you.

daily schedule chart. If more than one person is going to be responsible for walking the dog, make sure each person is clear when his or her designated walk time is. Many housetraining mistakes are due to the "I thought it was your turn to walk the dog" excuse.

CHEW-TOY TRAINING IN NO TIME

Have three prestuffed chew toys waiting for your new pup the minute he walks in the door. Immediately take him to his long-term confinement area and let him relax for a bit with his chew toys. This prevents several problems at once: Your new puppy will be learning to spend some quiet time on his own, he will begin his lifelong chew-toy habit, and he will learn to settle down quietly in the house.

SETTLE DOWN TRAINING

You will want an adult dog that can settle down when you're home and when you're not, so start teaching your little pup how to do this and he'll be a joy to live with from day one.

The quickest way to teach your pup to settle down is to tie his leash to a chair (or just step on it). Sit in the chair and ignore your dog until he settles quietly—then calmly praise him. If you are reading a book, get up and move to a different chair after every chapter. Bring the puppy with you and wait for him to settle down again. If you are watching TV, you can change seats every time a commercial comes on. This way he will learn that, even when people are around, settling down is a nice thing to do.

The pup must learn to settle down when you are home so he can learn to settle down when you aren't. But, be careful not to spend so much time with him that you set a precedent you can't continue. By showing a great deal of affection, you are basically saying to the puppy, "If you come into this house, you'll get attention all the time." You obviously can't keep this promise. The puppy is left feeling scared and anxious, and that isn't fair.

Teaching your puppy to enjoy his time alone is easy to do. Stuff two or three chew toys with some tasty morsels, place them and your dog in one of the two confinement areas, and presto! He will settle down and focus intently on his toys.

IT'S TIME TO SOCIALIZE!

Your puppy's socialization agenda should be well underway before you even get him. Check with the breeder to make sure the pup was raised indoors with lots of environmental stimulation and lots of human contact.

Nobody Likes a Deadline

No one likes to hear "Time's up!" Let's face it, though, deadlines are a fact of life. There are a number of socialization deadlines. By the time your puppy is 2 months old, for example, socialization with people must be well underway and desensitization to the physical environment must be virtually completed. This means your puppy should meet lots of people of varying age, race, and gender. He also should be exposed to variations in

A COMPLETE WASTE OF TIME

It's a waste of time to punish your puppy when you come home to a chewed-up house. From the dog's point of view, you are just punishing him for greeting you when you come home. The next time you return home, he may cringe, roll over, and pee in anticipation of you being mad at him.

his environment. If your puppy is properly environmen-
tally socialized, you will be hard pressed to find a sight or
sound that really scares him.

Your pup has lots to learn, but most importantly, he
must be socialized with people outside of your family. If
you wait until he is 3 months old to start, it will be much
harder.

Your puppy probably left his litter at around 8 weeks
old. One month from then (at the earliest), he can begin
to venture onto the streets with you to meet other dogs.
(The delay is because he is not yet immunized.) Make
sure you capitalize on this doggie social vacuum by focus-
ing on socializing your puppy with people. During this
time, have lots of people around the house hand feeding
and training so the puppy learns to love people. When
people are greeting your new puppy, it is a wonderful
opportunity to have them lure/reward train him. This
way, your pup is being socialized and trained at the same
time. How efficient! Visitors can teach the puppy loads of
things while you sit in your armchair with a cup of tea.
Check out the "Training Party" headings throughout the
book for some great ideas.

Socialization with people must be maximized by the
time your puppy is 3 months old. At this time, your puppy
should have met and positively interacted with as many
different people as possible—and I mean *as many*—close
to 100 is preferable. This shouldn't be too hard, he is a
puppy after all. It's not like you'll have to *beg* people to
come over and meet him!

By 3 months of age, your puppy is old enough to go outside. He also is ready to go to puppy class! Call the APDT or ask your veterinarian for a referral to a good class and get your little guy enrolled. Puppy classes are a blast! Not only will they be your pup's big night out, puppy classes also will be one of your most cherished memories of puppyhood before your puppy collides with adolescence.

At puppy classes, socialization with other dogs becomes a major priority, second only to continuing your puppy's enjoyable socialization with people. Continue to invite people over and take your puppy out as much as possible.

Though good and bad habits are pretty hard to change, socialization is not! You still need to continue to socialize the puppy throughout adolescence and adulthood. Whenever you stop walking your dog or letting him meet people and other animals, he will start to desocialize.

Just a Start on the Socialization Highway

The following are some lists to get you started socializing your dog. These lists are not comprehensive because there are too many aspects of socialization for one book. There are so many things that your dog should experience to learn to deal with the world in a languid manner. Every new, positive experience makes your dog that much more comfortable, sociable, and easy to share a life with. Be sure to at least expose your dog to everything listed below and hand feed lots of treats so your pup

Just as social interaction with people is important, so is your dog's interaction with other dogs. The simplest, most hassle-free way to help your dog make other doggie friends is to enroll him in puppy classes.

associates new people, places and things with something (food) he likes.

Environmental Socialization

- Radio and television playing
- Crowds of people
- Traffic
- Shopping malls
- Veterinary and grooming establishments

Socialization to People

- Men (of all ages and races)
- Women (of all ages and races)
- Children (of all ages and races)
- People in uniform
- People wearing hats
- People on bikes, skateboards, and skates
- Runners/joggers
- People talking loudly and screaming

Socialization to Other Animals

- Puppies
- Adult dogs
- Cats
- Other household pets
- Livestock

QUICK ⬤ PAINLESS

1. If you're a working person, consider having your puppy go to day care for the first two or three months of his life. At puppy day care, training is part of the routine daily program.

2. If you don't send your puppy to day care, consider getting a puppy sitter to come in at least a couple times a week to spend time with and train your puppy. This will help your pup go through adult life like a breeze.

TEACHING PEOPLE TO TEACH YOUR DOG

If you bring lots of people around during the puppy's first month at home, you can train those people to train your dog. Make sure to first inform visitors of the training tactics you are using. Don't just let them play with your puppy in an uneducated way.

If you recently redecorated your home, you would expect your friends to behave appropriately when visiting. You wouldn't want them ruining your home by spilling food on the floor or putting drink glasses on the table and leaving water ring marks. The same applies when they come over to visit your new pup. Teach them how to interact with him so they don't mess up his education. They may giggle when he jumps on them as a pup, but they won't like it when he is full grown. Give them a bag of his dinner kibble and show them how to lure him into a sit.

Usually only one person in a family trains a new puppy; the rest of the family members often wind up detraining him. One of the most important things for a puppy owner to learn is how to become a *people* trainer. Not only do you have to learn how to train the puppy, you also have to train all the people who come into contact with the puppy. If this is done effectively, you can just sit back in your armchair, relax, and simply watch the proceedings!

QUICK ◑ PAINLESS

Host lots of puppy parties in your home. Bring people into your home to train and socialize your puppy at the same time.

The critical period of socialization ends at 12 weeks of age. Expose your new puppy to as many people, places, and things as possible before that time.

Training Party: Puppy Welcoming Party

Never is the party method more appropriate than when you have a new puppy project. Invite a bunch of people with fancy hats and streamers to come over for party food and puppy games. This puppy needs to be totally socialized before he is 12 weeks old. As a rule of thumb, to be adequately socialized and to develop sufficient confidence and independence, your puppy needs to have been in contact with at least 100 people before he ventures outdoors at 3 months of age. Invite people over in droves so your puppy has a good time meeting lots of people in a friendly and structured setting.

The first item on the agenda is for guests to hand feed your pup. Hand feeding teaches the puppy to like people and people's hands. Instruct guests to handle the pup as they feed him, to reach for his collar and offer a treat, to handle his ears, to open his mouth, to hold his paws, to cradle him, and to hand feed, hand feed, hand feed! Frequent handling by strangers will put the pup in good standing for visits to the groomer or veterinarian.

Hand feeding also increases the value of kibble, which then can be used effectively as training treats to lure and reward your dog. Since you have guests, they might as well start training your puppy right away. Show your visitors how to teach your puppy to come, sit, lie down, and roll over (check out Chapter 10).

This is the most important example of how other people can do all the work for you. It is impossible to socialize your dog without enlisting the help of others. The easiest and quickest way to socialize a puppy is to entice him to approach and stay close—to come and sit. What better way to fit training into your schedule than to work it into your social life!?

ARMCHAIR TRAINING: SETTLE DOWN

With most dogs, there are really only three things to teach them— settle down, settle down, and settle down. The best way to do this is to have the puppy on a leash that is tied to a chair or that you are stepping on while you sit and read a book or watch the television. After every few pages or during commercial breaks, get up, move around a bit, and then come back to the chair and sit down. Your pup will learn to remain settled even though there is some activity. Periodically, move to another armchair and have the puppy settle down beside you. Your puppy will learn to settle down in a variety of spots and to settle down quickly.

This also is great to do when you begin to take your puppy for walks. Bring a good book or magazine with you when you take your puppy out. After he has eliminated and you are ready to take him for a little walk around the block (as a reward for eliminating), stop every few feet or so and ask your pup to settle down. This teaches your dog two things: to settle down (even when highly excited by the prospect of a walk around the block) and to relax a bit when you walk him. He will be less likely to pull on-leash because he knows he has to keep an eye on you to see when you will ask him to settle down again.

IF YOU'RE SO
INCLINED

You can teach your dog to settle down from your armchair, but if you really want to test his excitability, take your pet for a walk around the block or for a ride in a car. Training your dog to settle down in all situations will make it easier for you to gain control when you want to relax or when it's just not the right time for fun and games.

DOG TRAINS HIMSELF: CHEW TOY FEVER!

Always provide a number of chew toys whenever leaving your puppy in his short-term or long-term confinement area. The best chew toys are hollow. Stuff the chew toys with kibble or treats. Your pup will quickly teach himself to chew these chew toys, if only because there is nothing else to chew on that is as enticing. Indeed, within just a couple of days your puppy will become a veritable chew-toy-aholic! Now let's pause and ponder . . . If your puppy has developed a strong chew-toy habit and spends most of his time when left alone chewing on his chew toys, what isn't he doing? He isn't chewing inappropriate (costly and dangerous) household items, and he isn't barking. Brilliant!

Getting Time on Your Side

Everyone wants his or her puppy to be on good behavior. In order to achieve gold-star status, your puppy must be taught what is expected of him before he arrives in your home. This chapter emphasized the importance of choosing a puppy that has been well socialized by his breeder by the time you pick him up. You also know that your puppy's education should be well underway by the time he is 8 weeks old. If not, you are going to wind up with a very time-consuming training program. Getting your puppy to behave is also a treat with painless puppy training. You've learned to teach your puppy to tolerate time alone and to enjoy his settle-down time in his crate or by your side. Even suggestions for throwing training parties to teach other people to train your dog were added bonuses for those who have reached the pinnacle of lazy status!

Trouble-Free Ways to Teach a New Adult Dog Old Tricks

So you've decided to take the stress-free route—you're getting an adult dog. Good for you! If you take note of the following three pieces of advice, you will be able to train this dog with one hand tied behind your back:

1. Choose your new dog carefully.

2. Choose your new dog carefully.

3. Choose your new dog carefully.

As you can see, the real knack for having success with an adult dog is in the selection. Once again, here is a list of questions that will help you select the right dog:

1. How sociable is the dog with men, women, children, and other pets?

2. How interested in people is the dog? In a 20-minute test drive, how much attention does he pay to you and any other people in the room?

3. Is the dog fearful or overly rambunctious? (Either of these could be suitable for the right person.)

4. Does he know how to respond to requests such as sit, down, and come when called? If not, how quickly can you train him?

You can use the following two-step process to find out how trainable a dog is:

1. Ask yourself, "Do I know how to train an adult dog?" If the answer is "No," you need to hold off. You first should finish this book and sit in on a few good puppy- and dog-training classes in your area.

2. Determine whether the dog adapts to training. How do you check this out? Pick a motivator (such as treats, tennis balls, or squeaky toys) and show it to the dog. Once the dog likes something, he is trainable. If he doesn't like anything or if he isn't interested in you, he will probably need a specialist to train him, and he may not be the dog for you. Hold the motivator and do nothing. The dog will probably go through a repertoire of behaviors to get what you are holding. Ignore everything he does *unless* he sits. When he sits, give him a piece of food. Then take a step to get the dog active again— and wait again. Within about five minutes (at the most), you should have a sit-happy dog in front of

you! If you stay quiet and ignore everything the dog does other than sitting, he should catch on pretty quickly.

CRUISIN': TAKE YOUR DOG FOR A TEST DRIVE

Before you invite an adult dog into your family, take him for a little test drive. Taking a prospective new dog for a test drive is the best way to get a good idea of how suitable you are for each other. Sadly, there are loads and loads of dogs clamoring to be a member of your family. At the same time, however, this means there are lots of dogs from which to choose. Keep in mind that a dog that isn't suitable for your family may be perfect for another. The most important advice is to pick an adult dog that has a solid temperament and that fits in with your household and lifestyle.

No Surprises Here!

Many people go out, follow their heart, and end up with an unsuitable dog that actually wrecks the harmony in the household. The neat thing about getting an adult dog is that his behavior is pretty much fixed. You can select one that fits in with your lifestyle, that is house-trained and chew-toy trained, and that has some obedience training under his belt. It would be nice to find a dog that already knows what sit and settle down mean and that can walk nicely on-leash. When you test drive, look for these things. (This is not to say that you absolutely shouldn't get a dog if he doesn't know these

YOU'LL THANK YOURSELF LATER

Get an adult dog. With an adult dog, the first two weeks are very intensive but then you're pretty much done. A puppy, on the other hand, requires an enormous amount of energy for a few months and then even more energy to see him through adolescence.

things. It will make your life a little easier, however, if he does.) At the very least, you should teach the dog to do at least one thing before you bring him home.

There are many wonderful, teachable adult dogs waiting for great homes. It's not like there is a shortage of dogs out there.

When looking to adopt an adult dog, remember that both his temperament and his behavior repertoire are already pretty much fixed. You can select a dog you like, and he likely will remain as he is when you adopt him for quite some time—especially if you take the same precautions as you would with a new puppy for the first few weeks that the adult dog is home. This will set the precedent for many years to come.

Easy as 1-2-3 (and 4)

1. Another difference when getting an adult dog is that he is going to be out on the street right away. (Remember, puppies have to wait until they have their shots.) You should make sure the dog walks nicely on-leash. (See Chapter 16, "Lazy Luke Leashwalker.") It's important to realize that the dog is excited to be out of the shelter and is so ebullient and enthusiastic and crazy that he will pull on-leash—this sets the precedent for how you will walk on the street. When you go out for the first time, don't go anywhere. You don't have to walk the dog. Just bring him outside and stand around with him. Get him to understand that walking with you down the street is just that—walking *with* you. You can do

Contact a trainer right away. Either have that person train the dog for you and show you how it works or, even better, have him show you how to train your dog right in your own home.

The Lazy Way

this by making sure he watches you to see when you take a few steps and when you stop. The more time you spend with your dog just hanging around outside and not going very far, the less likely he is to act like a high-powered rocket when you go for walks. Many people think you should walk a dog mainly for the physical exercise. This is rubbish. You will never exercise a dog sufficiently by walking him. If you do walk for exercise, you are only training him to need even more walking to fully exercise himself. Physical exercise is a big aspect of walking, of course, but the psychological exercise for the dog is much more important. Just standing on the sidewalk with the dog on-leash is a wonderful event for the dog. He is in a completely new environment with all new smells and voices and things to see. So don't go anywhere. Just hang out. Let him take it all in. Wait until he settles a bit and then take a few steps. Stop again to let him settle again. He will quickly learn that relaxing is the best way to continue the all-important walk.

2. If you are getting an adult dog that is, say, 2 years old, the second thing to check is whether he can spend time home alone. The tendency with a new dog is, of course, to shower him with attention. All this does is camouflage some of the more serious behavior problems for about a week. The first thing you should do is bring the dog in, give him a stuffed chew toy in his bed, and have him settle down.

If you think that you need to constantly be walking and moving around with your dog to provide him with a sufficient amount of stimuli, think again. Dogs love just hanging out, which is great for the lazy trainer. So go ahead and relax on a lawn chair, while your dog happily takes in the change in scenery.

The Lazy Way

Remember, he is going to be left at home alone a lot. If he is interested in the chew toy while you are in the room, try leaving the room for a minute or so. If you've done a good job in stuffing that toy with something really tasty, chances are he won't pay much attention to the fact that you've left. When you can leave the room for 5 or 10 minutes without him losing interest in his toy, try to leave the house for a minute. Make sure your departures are as unexciting as possible. Avoid trying to reassure the dog that you'll be back soon. It's usually better for you to act like it's no big deal so that he won't think it is.

3. Within two to three days, you should know whether this dog is housetrained. That isn't to say you should allow him to roam around the house unsupervised. (That isn't safe for him or for your house!) Give him access to rooms only when you're with him. When you can't be there, have him in a crate or a long-term confinement area.

4. In the first week, have people over to train the dog. One option is to host a sit-to-greet party. (See the project at the end of this chapter.) This will give you a good idea how well socialized the dog is to different types of people. It also will actually be socializing him at the same time.

So, What's the Score?

If you've been marking off your test-drive list, by the end of the week you should have a pretty good idea how

YOU'LL THANK YOURSELF LATER

Choose an adult dog more for his behavior than for his looks. Beauty fades, but a good temperament is forever!

suitable this dog is for you (and vice versa). This process takes up only a week of your life, but it is going to be very intensive. Is this dog going to work out before you totally give him your heart? If not, you are in for a huge heartbreak.

PARTY TRAINING: HAND FEED THAT DOG

As previously mentioned, you can invite people over to hand feed and test drive the dog for you. It's good to get a number of independent opinions during the first three days the dog is home and *before* you make a commitment. Have your friends test out the dog—they should have him come, sit, lie down, walk on-leash, and all that sort of stuff. For adult dogs, however, the party usually is more of a welcome to the family and an excuse to invite people over to catch up on your social calendar.

ARMCHAIR TRAINING: BONDING TIME

Put your dog on-leash, sit in a chair, and read the newspaper. Basically, you should let the dog spend plenty of quiet time with you to bond. Most adult dogs are likely to be stressed in a new home, so don't blow him away during the first few days with over-the-top attention. Enjoy lots of quiet time—lots of armchair time. Maybe even spend time in a deck chair or a hammock in the back yard. Make sure you spend lots of time just sitting with your dog quietly relaxing in the same room and sometimes in another room in a confinement area,

IF YOU'RE SO INCLINED

When you take your dog for a walk, take some treats with you so you can work on socializing him while you are walking him down the street. Give a treat to each stranger that wants to say hi so he or she can give it to the dog when he sits.

IF YOU'RE SO
INCLINED

Get your adult dog involved in some fun dog-gie sports. Train him and take part in a Canine Good Citizen test, Obed-ience trials, Agility, fly-ball, and the list goes on . . . !

maybe even hand feeding him. Give him plenty of time to relax and to bond. This really will form the foundation for a good relationship.

You probably won't know what happened to this poor doggie in his past life. It probably hasn't been great or you wouldn't be taking him in. On the other hand, his previous life might have been grand until some terrible trauma, such as the death of his owner. This is your opportunity to correct those things.

DOG TRAINS HIMSELF (OR, DOG TRAINS YOU!)

Another neat thing about most adult dogs is that, if you take the time to pick a good one (one that is free of an overabundance of behavior and temperament prob-lems), the dog will train you. It's a brilliant thing. What is even more brilliant is that you won't even know you are being trained. It's effortless. You might be sitting in an armchair watching TV and your dog will come up and nuzzle. Without even knowing it, without it ever approaching conscious thought, you will get up and open the door to let him out to pee. Then you will just get up to let him back in again. If it hasn't happened yet, just wait . . . it will.

For better or for worse, keep your eyes open. An older dog certainly has had a lot of practice training owners. He will soon attempt to train you whenever he wants dinner, needs someone to open a door, or wants to be taken for a walk.

Getting Time on Your Side

What happens if you are truly bogged down and too busy to train a puppy, but don't want to miss out on the love and companionship of a great pet? With *The Lazy Way* you don't have to. That's why this chapter includes advice on adopting adult dogs. But just because you've decided to take this stress-free route doesn't mean there aren't important tips you need to know. You found great ways to choose an adult dog that's right for you. You went cruisin' with different dogs during test-driving sessions and found the pet that fits all your criteria. You discovered how sociable the dog is with men, women, children, and other pets, and if he responds to basic requests such as sit, down, and come when called. Now you can give an adult dog a second chance by using the lazy bonding techniques and giving lots of love. Isn't that what friends are for?

Hassle-Free Housetraining

Housetraining can be hassle-free, whether you calm your dog by having him lay down by your side for quiet time until you take him to his designated toilet, whether you train him by having him spend time in his properly constructed doggie den, whether you have a group of friends help train him, or whether you use a combination of all three. Although there are slight differences in how you housetrain an adult dog and a puppy, both can be simple and expedient.

YOUR FIRST HOUSETRAINING MISTAKE

Aside from watching the *Sirius Puppy Training* video, a good ol' dog walk is probably the most exciting event in your dog's daily life. Your dog likely looks forward to its beginning and loathes its ending. Walking a dog to stimulate him to pee or to poop generally becomes a *major* training error—one that can generate a number of problems.

Most smart dogs (and indeed, most are smarter than their owners in this respect) quickly learn that their highly enjoyable walk is highly likely to end the moment they deposit any kind of excretory product on the sidewalk. From here on out, your dog is likely to use delay tactics to postpone the end of his walk. This can be frustrating in itself.

Even more annoying, though, stemming from the fact that a dog's patience and determination usually exceed that of his owner, is that the dog's power to withhold might exceed the length of the walk. This is a big problem—the owner then returns home with a full dog that really needs to relieve himself.

Consequently, many dogs develop the habit of soiling the house immediately after returning home from a good, long walk. Ironically, the behavior effectively has been trained, albeit unintentionally, by the owner.

Luckily, the solution is simple and will save you loads of time and energy in the long run. Take your dog outside to relieve himself, but don't go anywhere! Just stand with your dog on-leash outside the entrance to your house or apartment building. Bring along a nice book and give your dog 10 minutes to produce.

If he doesn't go in the allotted time period, it's no big deal. Go back inside and try again in 30 minutes or an hour. During this time, keep an eye on your dog by having him on a leash at your side or in his short-term confinement area.

If the dog does eliminate while standing outside, this is wonderful. Let him know it's wonderful! Tell him "What a wonderful doggie! Do you want to go for walkies?"

Clean up the mess, dispose of it, say "walk" once more, and proceed to enjoy walking your empty dog.

Rather than punishing your dog by ending the walk and starting for home the minute he relieves himself, you are now starting the walk by rewarding him for prompt delivery. You'll find that a no-feces-or-urine, no-walk policy produces a speedy on-command eliminator within just a few days of training. The walk itself becomes the reward!

PUPPY HOUSETRAINING

Until your puppy is at least 3 months old, he will need to eliminate quite often. Puppies are pretty predictable—they need to go as soon as they wake up, after they have played, shortly after eating or drinking, and just about every couple hours (at least!). If you devise a feeding, watering, confinement, and walking schedule for your puppy's day, it is very easy to predict when he needs to make a potty run.

Train Your Dog to Go on Cue

This is no different from training your dog to do anything else—such as sit, lie down, or roll over—on cue. The training sequence is the same:

1. Ask the dog to do it.

2. Lure the dog to do it.

3. When he does it, praise him, pet him, and give him a treat.

The only real difference is that, with housetraining, you won't be luring the dog to eliminate. Instead, you

YOU'LL THANK YOURSELF LATER

Confinement, confinement, confinement. The most important part of housetraining, whether you are training a puppy or an adult dog, is preventing him from making a mistake. Make sure you train your dog to come into the home and go right to his area. This area should be specifically designed to encourage the dog either to go in a specific doggie toilet (for puppies) or to hold it until you take him out for a walk (for adult dogs).

need to predict when he needs to go. Basically, this is a crate-training routine. What's important is the first thing you do, even before motioning that you are going to take the dog outside. You should say "Hey, let's go pee, let's go pee!" You then take the dog out of his crate and into the backyard or out to the front of the house on-leash. Just wait for him to go—he certainly will want to if he has been confined in his crate or sleeping for an hour or two. When he does go, say "Good puppy!" and give him a treat. After a dozen or so repetitions, the dog will figure out that, when you say "Hey, let's go pee and poop," it is his chance to urinate and defecate—and, of course, to get some liver treats.

Bull's-eye! Training Your Dog to Go in a Very Specific Spot

Training your dog to consistently go potty in one specific area is very useful for people who have very small backyards and who don't want the dog eliminating all over the place. It also is good for people who walk their dog on the street and who want him to learn to go in a certain spot as soon as they go outside. You will really appreciate this on cold or rainy nights!

Put your dog on-leash (even if you are taking him into the backyard) and stand still right by his toilet. Give him three minutes to go. If he does, give him a liver treat. If he doesn't, take him back inside for another 45 minutes of supervision or confinement.

Another way to do this is to set up a concentration gradient for the rewards the dog gets. Imagine the doggie toilet is the bull's eye of a target. If he gets within, say, 10 yards, he gets a "Good boy!" Even though he missed, it's better than him doing it inside. If he gets within 5 yards, say "Good boy!" twice and maybe pat him on the head. If he gets within 3 yards, he gets lots of enthusiastic praise *and* a liver treat. If he hits ground zero, he gets three liver treats. This is a game your dog will enjoy playing, and he will work it out very quickly. He can become as particular about picking his elimination spot as a cat!

PARTY TRAINING: FUN WITH HOUSETRAINING

Until the puppy is 3 or 4 months old, you might want to get some puppy sitters to housetrain him at home. It's just the most effortless way to do it. These people can take the puppy out to the doggie toilet every hour on the hour. If he goes, they will give him three liver treats. The pup will catch on so quickly that, eventually, he will rather bust his bladder than soil the house. This really is a case to elicit help. The puppy sitters can walk the puppy, as long as they know how to do it.

Make sure your people get trained before they train your pup. Likely candidates are surprisingly easy to find—perhaps a next door neighbor or an elderly person who would like to have a dog but can't.

QUICK ◼ *PAINLESS*

It is important to positively reinforce your dog. Using words and gestures of praise can facilitate training and teach your dog that obeying commands is rewarding and fun.

ARMCHAIR TRAINING: HOUSETRAIN FROM YOUR CHAIR

Believe it or not, while sitting in an armchair, you can housetrain your puppy. Just have the pup on a leash sitting beside you. Puppies are filled with energy. You've got to teach them to settle down much more than you would an adult dog, for a number of reasons. With the puppy, of course, the level of activity is out of control! You want to let the puppy know that quiet little moments are an essential ingredient of day-to-day living.

While in an armchair, start off by having the puppy settle down next to you. Then have him settle down in a crate or on a tie-down in another room so that he doesn't get used to always being next to you. This produces a calmer puppy, a puppy that adjusts well to times when he is left home alone.

Most importantly, if you have your puppy settle down and every hour on the hour you take him outside, he is going to urinate within minutes if not seconds of getting outside. This is what you're going for. Training your puppy to settle down is the only way you can successfully predict when he wants to urinate and defecate. And, of course, the only way you can direct the proceedings is to take him outside and then give him liver treats for going where he's supposed to go.

DOG TRAINS HIMSELF: HANDS-OFF HOUSETRAINING

Your puppy/dog can housetrain himself if you set up the appropriate living situation. The ideal here is a puppy that has a very comfortable bedroom or doggie den—something the size of a dog crate with a cozy blanket in it—with access to an outside toilet. This could be a dog flap through a wall in the kitchen to an outdoor run. The crate should be flush against the dog-door flap so that, when you are away from home, he is housed in this area. He has his very comfy bedroom with his toys, water, and bed, and all he has to do is go through the dog flap (which he will) to urinate and defecate. The puppy's basic instincts will train him to eliminate as far as possible from his bed.

When you are at home, you have the option to open the inside door of the dog crate that opens into the kitchen. If you have a stuffed chew toy tied to the inside of his crate, your pup will happily lie down there most of the time. The pup already has autoshaped, or self-trained, himself to use the outside as a toilet.

One thing to keep in mind—even though the toilet is outside, keep it clean. Feces need to be picked up every day. You'll find that the first day the dog defecates it will be towards the end of the run—far, far away from the bed. If you clean it up, the dog will do it there day after day. If you don't, each day the dog will defecate a little closer to the house. Dogs don't like to defecate where there already are feces.

As discussed before, however, it is not as urgent to clean up a dog's urine. Urine scent in the dog's toilet actually is good because the dog will cover it the next day. In fact, the more urine there is, the more he will urinate in that spot. You probably will want to clean up the

Install a dog-door flap in your door and keep your dog's crate flush against the flap so your dog will instinctively eliminate outside (as far away from his doggie bed) while he is home alone.

The Lazy Way

urine for the sake of human noses, however, just so it doesn't stink. This is okay because you'll never clean it up so much that the dog's nose won't pick it up. The dog will know he has peed there—it's as simple as that.

Dog owners who do not have access to a yard should set up the dog's crate in one corner of the bathroom, kitchen, utility room, or garage and should cover the rest of the floor with newspaper.

You might want to further reduce the pup's papered area by placing the crate in a small (6' × 6') exercise pen. This setup will quickly autoshape the dog to use papers, which then can be taken on walks both as a substrate stimulus for the dog to eliminate and to facilitate cleanup. Eventually, you won't have to use the paper in the confinement area, and the dog will only eliminate outdoors.

THE THREE WORST THINGS TO DO WHEN HOUSETRAINING YOUR DOG

The following are three examples of what not to do when housetraining:

1. *Don't* yell at your dog if you catch him making a mistake in the house. (If you do, next time your dog will wait until you're gone before building up the courage to relief himself.) Instead, be instructive and guide him outside.

2. *Don't* rub his nose in a mistake. Again, you'll only create a puppy that yearns to poop in private. You are creating the owner-absent house-soiling problem. In addition, this objectionable activity will only

grind the feces into the carpet, which will then need to be thoroughly cleaned—definitely not *The Lazy Way* to do things!

3. *Don't* make him stay in his crate if he messes in it. If you do, you are out of your mind! Who on earth would consider doing such a messy thing? And who is it that is going to bathe this dog, exactly? Hard work! Not *The Lazy Way*! Not *The Lazy Way* at all!

QUICK ⬤ PAINLESS

If you use punishment training to housetrain your dog, think of the thousands of wrong places where he can choose to eliminate. If you *reward* him for going in the *right* spot, however, training will be quicker and more pleasant for you both.

Getting Time on Your Side

Does your dog like to leave you doggie surprises behind the couch, under the bed, or in the corner of your dining room? Not anymore, now that you know *The Lazy Way* to hassle-free housetraining. You learned quick tips on teaching your dog to go on cue, and to eliminate in a very specific spot. And in some cases you didn't even have to go farther than your own armchair to do it. Now you know how to prevent your dog from soiling in the house immediately after returning home from walks. This chapter also gave you time-saving techniques to teach your dog to settle down and helped you understand why you should use positive reinforcement when housetraining your dog. With the lazy tips you've read you are now better equipped for teaching your pet to eliminate calmly and quickly. See, by doing it *The Lazy Way* you hardly had to put any effort into it at all—that means plenty of time that wasn't flushed down the toilet!

Eschew Chewing

Chewing is one of the most normal and necessary activities in which your dog will engage. The act of chewing isn't a problem. The problem is your dog's choice of chew toys (such as your living room furniture!). Many ill-informed owners try to teach their dogs by punishing them every time they chew on unsuitable objects. Apart from being unpleasant, this is an extremely inefficient way to train your dog, especially when you consider just how many unsuitable objects there are in the house. It's ridiculous—you'll be punishing the dog over and over and over before he learns which objects are suitable to chew on and which aren't.

Even more likely, though, after you've caught your dog in the act of chewing a few times and punished him for it, you'll have blown his entire education because from that moment on you will never be able to catch him in the act again. The dog will only chew when you are out of the way. He isn't stupid. Your punishments have simply taught him not to chew items when you're around. You will still have the problem, but it will be even worse. You'll have an owner-absent chewing problem. Not only did the punishment routine take a long

QUICK PAINLESS

1. Stuff six chew toys (or sterilized bones) with kibble or treats and put them in the fridge for later use. (Refrigeration keeps the stuffings fresh.)

2. Put a stuffed chew toy in your dog's crate. (This is your dog's version of TV!)

time, and not only was it unpleasant for the dog and for you—it didn't even work!

IT'S SIMPLE! SHOW HIM WHAT HE *CAN* CHEW ON

The smart way to teach a dog also is quick and easy. You have to teach him what you want him to chew on. Obviously, if your dog is happily engrossed in a chew toy, he will not be chewing inappropriate items. Your mission is to make sure that your dog thinks chew toys are just the best thing since sliced bread! You've got to make sure that, given all the items in the house, the one article the dog most likes to chew is his chew toy. Supply your dog with lots of chew toys and make them even more fun by playing lots of chew-toy games. You can do this by stuffing the chew toys with food, by hiding the dogs stuffed chew toys, or by letting them dangle on a length of string.

HE'S A CHEW-TOY-AHOLIC!

Turn your dog into a chew-toy-aholic by stuffing a few chew toys with different fillings such as dry kibble, peanut butter, or dog biscuits. Your dog will grow to *love* these. Simply stuff his chew toys with treats, and he will train himself to bite the toy and not the furniture!

Think of the many things your dog won't be able to do while engrossed in a chew toy. If your dog is chewing a chew toy, he will not be destroying household articles, he will not be running around the house getting into mischief, and he will not be barking. Hello, stuffed chew toy—bye-bye, behavior problems!

It's a simple fact, if your dog teaches himself to chew on a toy, there are a good hundred other things he can't be doing at the same time—most of them mischievous.

PARTY TRAINING: MUSICAL CHEW TOY

You want your dog to learn that chew toys are wonderful, so invite some friends over and have a chew-toy party!

It's time to play musical chew toy. This is a great game for children, and it has numerous benefits. Your dog gets trained by the children, and the children have a great time with the dog. The children also learn how to interact with the dog, and your dog learns to respect and like the children. To begin, designate one child as the disc jockey. Have each guest sit in a chair. As the music plays, pass the chew toy from person to person. When the music stops, the person with the chew toy has to train

QUICK ⬤ PAINLESS

Without being rude, a really simple solution to many chewing problems is to clean up your house. Make sure all destructible and valuable objects are out of the puppy's way. Put clothing in drawers and closets. Put the remote control out of reach on top of the television. Flush used paper tissues down the toilet. Have children clean up their toys. There is nothing better than shutting a few doors to limit your puppy's access to various rooms. You might want to roll up the carpets and hang the drapes out of reach until your puppy has gotten over his teething stage and until you have taught him a chew-toy habit. It only takes a couple minutes to prepare, and you'll spare yourself hours of cleanup time!

Give your new dog a
stuffed chew toy the
minute he arrives to
your house. The first
thing he will learn is
that little, quiet
moments are the status
quo in this household.
He'll also learn that
chew toys are the
chewing object of
choice. Make sure to
also give your dog a
couple of stuffed chew
toys every time you
leave him home alone.

the dog with it. Of course, the dog is used to having this chew toy stuffed with treats, so he will follow it like a treat. You can use any type of toy that can be stuffed with a tasty treat: a tennis ball cut open with a treat inside tied to a string, a sterilized bone, a hollow chew toy, and so on.

You also can play hide the chew toy. When the music stops, the person in whose hands the toy has landed has to get up. Someone holds the dog while the person hides the toy. Then the doggie gets to go and find it.

If the kids you know or your friends are a less-active bunch, you can just have some chew-toy-stuffing parties. Your guests can help you prepare the dog's toys for the week. You can use all sorts of items to stuff chew toys, so have a variety ready for the stuffing party. Try peanut butter, cheese, or a bit of meat. Weigh out some of your dog's weekly food, wet it to a mulch, and stuff some into the chew toys. In the summer, you can freeze them and make pupsicles for the dog.

ARMCHAIR TRAINING: FIND THE STUFFED CHEW TOY

When you come home from work, take a seat in your armchair and tell your dog to get his chew toy. Delay greeting your dog until he is holding his toy in his mouth. Say "Find your toy! Find your toy!" You may have to point at it a few times to help him get the idea. Once your dog finds his chew toy, lavish him with praise and affection. Hug him, kiss him, maybe even invite him to sit on your lap for a cuddle.

After a few days of you following this relaxing routine, your dog will develop the notion that, as the day goes on and it gets closer and closer to the time when you come home, he should get his chew toy, because that's what you're going to tell him to do anyway. Expecting you, he'll run for his toy and have it handy for you when you arrive so you can remove that little piece of freeze-dried liver that always is so difficult to extricate. This is, of course, a most convenient state of affairs because right before you come home is one of the peak times for a dog to chew up the house. He can't do that if he has a chew toy in his mouth, can he?

DOG TRAINS HIMSELF: SIMPLY STUFF

This is absolutely, positively the most exertion-free way to train your dog. Just stuff a few chew toys and hollow bones with treats, and your dog will train himself into a chew-toy-aholic. The choice between a piece of furniture and a tasty stuffed chew toy is an easy one.

It is still advisable, however, to supervise your dog until you know he is really obsessed with his designated chew toys. For times when you can't be with him, confine him to his long-term confinement area with a couple of stuffed chew toys.

A COMPLETE WASTE OF TIME

As with housetraining, it is counter-productive to punish your dog if you come home to find that he has chewed the place up. This only teaches your dog to dread you coming home. This will, of course, cause him to become extremely stressed. He will probably indulge in this habitual behavior even more (as a stress reliever) when he expects you to come home.

Most destructive chewing happens right after the owner leaves (usually out of relief) and right before the owner comes back home (dreading the owner's return). Always remember, when you punish your dog when you come home, he will learn to dread your return (gee, I wonder why!).

Getting Time on Your Side

Chew on this: Your dog's tendency to chew anything he can sink his teeth into is totally normal and necessary behavior. This chapter has advised you to stop spending valuable time trying to prevent your pup from chewing because it's what he chews on that counts. Introducing your dog to the all-purpose chew toy is the key to keeping your valuables from falling victim to gnawing jaws. You no longer find holes in your shoe soles and your telephone wire is still intact because you have discovered *The Lazy Way* to make chew-toy training enjoyable for you and your dog. Maybe you've even gone a bit overboard since your dog became a chew-toy-aholic and would rather be playing with his bone or liver-stuffed toy than hanging out with you. Can you really blame him?

Sit, Down, Stand, and Stay Awhile

The age-old lure/reward training method has made a dramatic comeback. Lure/reward methods are as old as the hills. In fact, they're so old, they're new again! Lure/reward techniques remove the need for physical coercion and corrections, enabling family and friends (children included) to train your dog. It's almost magic—the dog follows the lure and learns to sit, lie down, and stand. This all happens in a matter of seconds!

Dogs enjoy this type of training so much that, if you had the time and the desire, you could train them at least 50 times a day without them getting bored. That doesn't mean you have to do so, however. Instead, just weigh out your dog's dry kibble in the morning and get different people to hand feed and train him throughout the day. How do you do this? Go back to the good ol' party, of course!

With lure/reward training, you can teach all three commands at once. The dog will learn them all—at lightning

Your dog will sit in no time if you use a treat as a combination lure and reward. Simply guide him into position holding the treat, and when he's there, reward him with it! Gooood dog!

speed. Lure/reward methods are tailor-made for training young puppies, and they are the method of choice for re-educating older dogs.

Lure/reward training is easy and effortless. Simply take a piece of your dog's kibble and hold it in front of his nose. If you move the kibble up and down and your dog nods his head, this means your dog can't wait to start training. He is interested in the kibble, and the kibble works well as both a lure *and* a reward.

It will eventually become possible to move the lure to show the dog what you want him to do. Offer him the kibble as a reward afterward to thank him for doing it.

The routine is simple when training any command:

1. Tell the dog what to do.

2. Move the lure so the dog can work out what you want him to do.

3. When the dog follows your instructions, praise him and maybe even offer the food lure as a reward.

For example, when training the sit command:

1. Say "Rover, sit!"

2. Move the lure (kibble) backwards over your dog's muzzle. Aim right between his eyes and between his ears. Your dog will look up to follow the kibble. Keep the lure very close to his head, or he will jump up to grab it. As your dog follows the kibble, he will move his head back, look up, and then sit down.

3. As soon as his rear end hits the ground, say "Good dog, Rover!" and give him the treat.

See, training is as simple as 1-2-3!

Next try to teach your dog the down command. With your dog sitting, waggle the food in front of his nose and:

1. Say "Rover, down!"

2. Holding the lure between your finger and thumb with your palm down, move your hand straight down to the ground between the dog's forepaws. His nose will go down to the ground to follow the lure. Gently draw the lure slowly away from his paws so he stretches out his neck to follow the lure. At this point, your dog will either lie down or stand up.

3. If your dog lies down, well done! Say "Good dog!" and give him the piece of kibble as a reward. If your dog stands up, don't worry—just do it again. He will soon get the idea. The first time he does, he'll quickly realize he is onto a good thing. He will quickly grasp the idea that following the lure to the ground and laying down is rewarding; standing up is not. To increase the likelihood that your dog will lay down, move the food downward between his paws very quickly but then away from him very slowly. Keep it hidden under your hand so the dog has to put the side of his muzzle on the ground to get the treat.

An alternative luring technique that works well with young puppies—especially on a slippery floor—is to waggle the food in front of the puppy's nose when he is sitting. Say "Down!" and quickly lower the food straight

IF YOU'RE SO
INCLINED

Depending on how big your dog is, you may need to kneel or sit beside him while teaching him the down. No problem—then you're right there to tell him what a good boy he is when he's mastered the task.

down between her forepaws, but then slowly push the lure towards her belly. Usually, your puppy will slide her hindquarters backwards as he lowers her head to the lure, and he will plop into a down.

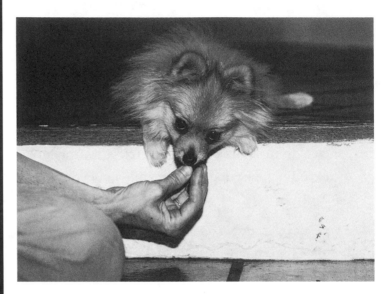

Working on a table or a step can make lure/reward training easier for dogs with short legs.

Yet another method to lure your dog down is to get him to crawl under a coffee table. Your dog will have to lie down before crawling under the low-slung coffee table. Once he is under the table, keep the lure still. You will get a brilliant down-stay. Another alternative is to lure your dog to crawl under your leg while sitting on the floor.

Believe it or not, there are still more little tricks to make luring your dog into a down happen as quick as a snap. For short legged or little dogs, try luring on a staircase. Position your dog on the top step, and yourself about two steps down. Show your dog the lure and move your hand straight down to the next step.

How about getting your dog to stand!? Whether your dog is sitting or lying down:

1. Say, "Rover, stand!"

2. Move the lure away from your dog's nose to the point where his nose would be if he stood up (which, of course, he will do because he wants to get the food). As soon as your dog stands, lower the kibble just a tad. Otherwise, your dog will stand and then immediately sit again.

3. When your dog stands, say "Good dog" and, if you like, offer a food reward.

It is a good idea to alternate the three positions—sit, down, and stand. These three body positions are the building blocks of training. Once your dog will quickly sit, lie down, and stand, you can do pretty much anything with him. This means you can get him to be calm, to focus, to get a grip on life, and to pay attention to you. Practicing any of these three positions teaches your dog to be still and focus on you.

PUPPY PUSH-UPS

Try little training sequences such as a sequence of puppy push-ups—sit and then down, sit again and then down, and so on. See how many puppy push-ups you can get your puppy to do for just one piece of kibble, or see how many push-ups your adult dog can do in 30 seconds.

IF YOU'RE SO INCLINED

Sit, down and stand are the building blocks of training. When your dog's got them figured out, vary the order in which you ask him to do them. This'll keep you both interested and thinking.

You also can practice a sequence such as sit, down, sit, stand, down, stand. Most people teach sit, down, and stand as three separate exercises. In actual fact, however, you are trying to teach the dog six different position changes: sit from a stand, down from a sit, sit from a down, stand from a sit, down from a stand, and stand from a down.

Practice all these positions and, after just one week, your dog will be moving at lightning speed and paying lots of attention to you to see what's coming next—will it be sit, stand, or down? This is one of the biggest secrets of training. Once your dog has learned to respond quickly and happily to these commands, everything else will be easy as pie.

Use a lure to guide the dog's body to lie down.

Using food lures is so much easier and quicker than physically guiding or forcing a dog to lie down. Also, the dog enjoys this technique!

By raising the lure upward and backward along the top of the dog's muzzle, the dog will look up and then sit down.

YOU'LL THANK YOURSELF LATER

Don't forget to teach your dog to stand. This is a great utilitarian command—if your dog is standing, you can groom him. And, of course, every veterinarian loves a dog that can stand for examination. In addition, if you teach your dog to stand, he will learn to pay better attention to you to see which of the six position changes you ask for next.

Teach your dog that sitting is the default setting for any scenario and your dog will virtually be problem-free.

QUICK  PAINLESS

Once your dog knows what "Stand" means, you can ask him to do it at the veterinarian's, the groomer's, when children want to pet him—everyone will love your well-behaved dog.

Training your dog to enjoy standing still is an underrated command. In actual fact it has many, many uses. Your veterinarian and groomer will love you for it!

PUNISHMENT: A TOTAL WASTE OF TIME

Jerking a dog, pushing him, and *any* kind of physical prompting is a complete waste of time. All you will be teaching your dog is to respond to prompts. (In lieu of verbal commands, touching the dog on the butt prompts him to sit down.) This works brilliantly if he is sitting next to you, but when he is 5 feet away, you have no control over him.

At home, your dog usually is off-leash and wandering around the house most of the time. When you're sitting in an armchair and your dog is about to jump on the kids in the kitchen, you want to be able to say "Sit!" and have him do it. You want your dog to listen to the words you say. Therefore, you should lure/reward train your dog from the outset.

One feature of this method is that it can be done off-leash (in a safe, enclosed area). You give no physical prompting cues to the dog. Instead, the dog has to use his brain to learn what the verbal instructions mean. Keep your hands off the dog during training! Once the dog is trained, of course, you should use your hands to pet him and reward him for getting it right.

FOOD FOR THOUGHT

If you're thinking you want your dog to sit, stand, and down simply because you told him to, or that if you use food your dog will get fat or only do it for the food, think again. First, regardless of popular opinion, no dog is born with the desire to please humans. Dogs are living

YOU'LL THANK YOURSELF LATER

When you teach any sequence of commands, for the dog to really understand what each command means, you have to teach at least three at a time. If you just teach sit and down, for example, all the dog learns is "If I'm sitting and they say something, then I lay down to get a cookie." If you teach three at a time and the dog is sitting, however, the dog doesn't know whether to lay down or to stand to get the reward. This makes the dog focus a little more on what you say or on the hand signals you give.

Don't let your dog get fat by indulging him in too many training treats. Instead, ration out some of his breakfast or dinner kibble and use that to train him throughout the day.

creatures with their own agenda. They do things because of how it makes them feel (if a behavior results in something good they'll do it again), not because of how you feel. Dogs will start to do things for your praise, but only after you have developed a good relationship (part of which has to do with your dog learning food comes from you). Second, if you are concerned your dog will get fat if you use too many treats, then don't. Just use the dog's normal meal kibble. Instead of giving him his total daily ration of food in a bowl, use each piece (or at least some of them) to train him throughout the day. Third, if you're worried your dog will only listen to you if you have food, fear not. After a few days of training your dog by using a piece of kibble or treat as a lure and reward for each position you should start asking your dog to do more for each piece (i.e. for one piece your dog must sit, down, sit, stand, and down). Also, you should put the food or toy in your pocket and ask the dog to do something, then take it out to reward. After a few days of doing this you don't even have to have the reward on your body. Instead, teach your dog that if he does what you ask you have the ability to sometimes go over to the cupboard and pull out a tasty treat or a favorite toy. But, he never knows when you will do this so he keeps trying.

STAY

Stay doesn't have to be a separate command. In fact, it probably shouldn't be. After all, what do we mean when we ask our dog to sit, stand, or down? To do so and get up after a second? I don't think so. Just teach your dog that when you ask him for one of the three body positions it means to do so and stay there until released or asked to do something else. This makes things much easier for you and your dog. Anyway, what good is it to have a dog that needs you to have your hand up, saying "Stay, stay, stay?" What if you asked him to sit so you can go answer the door? This isn't very convenient.

Please Don't Release Me

If taught properly, the release word will be something your dog doesn't want to hear. What it will come to mean is the ending of praise and rewards. First, choose a word (lots of people use "All done" or "Okay"). Ask your dog to sit or down. Count to three and praise your dog lavishly for being in a position. Then, say your release word and ignore the dog when he gets up. In a couple of seconds ask the dog to do sit or down. Again, give lots of praise and treats for being in the position and release the dog in a boring manner. Pretty soon you'll have a dog that is begging you to ask him to sit, stand, or down.

Remember to release your dog from positions with the release word. For each time you ask him for a sit, stand, or down and let him choose when to get up, you are teaching him that he doesn't have to stay. Also, be sure to praise him and reward him when he is in a position and make the release a boring affair.

There are three components to teaching your dog to stay when you say sit, stand, or down; length of time in the position, distance from you, and distractions while in each position. Work on each separately to make things easy on you and the dog.

YOU'LL THANK YOURSELF LATER

Don't forget to use your release word to excuse your dog from a particular command. If he learns he can break from what you've asked him to do before you say it's OK, you'll have to start over again.

Will Work for Food

All you have to do to teach your dog to stay for a longer period of time is simply delay giving him the piece of kibble. Say "Rover, sit" and hold the kibble for the count of three, then give it to him. Next time ask him to sit and hold onto the kibble for the count of five, then give the kibble and some praise and release. You will be proudly showing off your superbly trained dog in a matter of days.

The power of cookie training is to see how long you can hang on to a single piece of kibble. How many separate behaviors and responses can you get a dog to do for just one food reward? Or how long can you get the dog to stay in the same position for a single food reward? These are fun party games.

DISTANCE MAKES THE HEART GROW FONDER

Even an 8-week-old puppy can be taught to do position changes from a distance. Once your dog is a master position changer just a foot or so in front of you start working on distance commands. Tie your dog to something stationary. Take a step or two away and hold a piece of kibble in your hand as you use the same hand and voice signals to lure your dog into each position. Take a step in to give the dog the kibble each time he changes to the position you asked for. Within minutes you should be able to get your dog to sit, stand, and down from a few feet away. Within a week you should be able to do so from across a room. Have a contest to see which family

QUICK ⬥ PAINLESS

Now that your buddy knows what he needs to do to get that treat from you, start asking him for more—sit and then down before getting a treat, sit then stand before getting a treat. He's putty in your hands!

member can get the dog to change positions from the farthest distance.

DISTRACTIONS, DISTRACTIONS

Your dog is now a superb position changer (and stayer) in your home. But, pretty soon you are going to want to venture outside to show off to your friends and neighbors. But what about all those distractions, like kids running by and squirrels? Not to fear, proofing is here! Get out a piece of paper and list from 1 to 10 (in order of importance) your dog's favorite things and/or the things that most distract him. For my dogs the list goes something like this:

1. Squirrels

2. Food

3. Other dogs

4. Squeaky toys

5. Me (If I were being honest I would probably be in sixth place!)

6. Playful children

7. Friendly people

8. Tennis balls

9. Stuffed chew toys

10. Fast-moving people (joggers, in-line skaters, bikers)

When proofing your dog to distractions, it is helpful to have someone to assist you. Starting with number 10 (the lowest-ranking distraction), ask your dog to do some

IF YOU'RE SO
INCLINED

Start proofing your dog in the face of distractions. Figure out what gets to him most, then train him with the distraction 30 to 40 feet away. This will not only be a test of how well trained he is, but how interesting you are. Make it fun!

position changes with that distraction about 20 to 30 feet away. If you can succeed in doing so, move the distraction a little bit closer to you and ask the dog to do some sit, down, stand position changes again.

HAND SIGNALS

Humans communicate using the spoken or written word. To teach a dog the meaning of a single word can take a long time. Dogs, however, can learn facial expressions and body movements—just like that!

It is extremely easy for a dog to learn hand signals—so let's try training with them! (A lure should be used with the hand signals, so be sure to have it in hand!)

The hand signal for sit is a sweeping movement of the hands in front with palms up. For down, use a sweeping downward movement with your palms down. "Stand" is a movement of your hand straight out to the side. This is great because you can have already taught these signals using lure/reward training. Now just do it without a piece of food in your hand. Just remember to randomly produce a bit of kibble and some praise as a reward. When you go to the park and silently give hand signals to your dog, these signals are easy for your dog to understand, but onlookers will be really impressed.

Train little but often. Even if you had the time, lengthy training sessions would probably bore *you* as much as your dog. You'll be happy to know it's important to keep your training sessions extremely short—only a few seconds long—but to work with your dog many, many times each day. Try to integrate training into your

A COMPLETE WASTE OF TIME

The following are three ways to waste your time:

1. Feeding your dog out of his bowl everyday (not only a waste of time, but a waste of food lures and rewards)

2. Not asking your dog to do something before you give him his food

3. Allowing your dog to eat his food without interruption

TRAIN YOUR DOG The Lazy Way

regular lifestyle. This way, you will not be spending any extra time training your dog. You can train your dog, for example, every time you go into the kitchen, every time you turn a page of the newspaper, and every time you open a door for him. It is surprisingly easy to train your dog as many as 50 times a day—without ever deviating from your normal schedule!

PARTY TRAINING: EXERCISE PARTY!

From the time your dog is 8 weeks old until well into his sunset years, you want people to come to your house for dog-training parties. Invite family and friends to the house. You can get everyone into the swing of things by having training competitions and by awarding ribbons and other prizes. This will quickly get people motivated to work with your dog.

Congratulations! You got your dog to sit when inside the house! Now take a break and take a walk in the park to show off your well-behaved pooch. Be sure to bring along some toys and treats and ask him to sit some more.

One of the best ploys in training is to invite friends over and to show them how to train your dog for you.

Time people doing sit-down-stand repetitions or see who can get the dog to perform the most doggy push-ups (sit-downs) in a minute. You also can have competitions to see who can get the dog to do the longest stay (within reason, of course!).

You also can have competitions between two dogs (as in, the first dog in the down position gets the treat). Dogs *and* owners love it.

ARMCHAIR TRAINING: GET HIM TO SIT WHILE YOU'RE SITTING

Be relaxed, have a cup of tea, and train your dog from an armchair or couch a little bit at a time and often. Every time there are commercials on the television, for example, you can call your pup over for a couple seconds of action-packed position changes. You can do this when working on the computer, when lying in a hammock in the yard, when preparing dinner, or anywhere. Got the picture? Numerous ultra-short training sessions throughout the day can help develop your dog into a happy, willing student.

DOG TRAINS HIMSELF: HE'LL DO IT ON HIS OWN

Dogs learn many things on their own without much, if any, interaction from us. Think of your dog out in the yard—he hears a funny hissing sound coming from the grass. He walks over to investigate and, in a flash, he is sprayed with water. After just one trial, your dog will figure out that the hiss is a warning that the yard sprinkler is about to go on.

Similarly, your dog can learn just as quickly what you want him to do without you even having to say a word. Your dog can learn to sit, lie down, stand, and stay in certain situations without you doing much more than standing in front of him. Your only job is to reward anything he does that you like.

Hold a piece of kibble, stand still, and watch the dog. If he sits or lies down, give him the treat. Take a step away to entice the dog to stand and follow you, then wait for him to sit or lie down again. Repeat this over and over. You will find that, eventually, your dog will sit instantaneously after each step.

Reward training is a lovely way to allow your dog to work out what you want. Your dog knows you have treats and he wants them, so he will likely run through his complete behavioral repertoire until he finds the behaviors that get you to offer him food. It's as if the dog views you as a massive food vending machine and he has to work out which buttons to press to receive food payouts. This is a very effective technique to train rapid sits and downs and a terrific way to teach your dog to walk nicely on-leash.

You'll get to a point with your dog where you won't have to do anything: He'll want the treat and will perform for you to get it. How easy is that?!

The Lazy Way

Getting Time on Your Side

When it comes time to teach your dog basic good manners—and these include sit, down, stand, and stay awhile—it doesn't hurt to enroll in a puppy or basic training class. However, you can take the time it would normally take to get in the car and go to class just one night a week and use it to simply and effectively train at home. Just use the food you would normally serve your dog at one meal and practice the surefire lure/reward methods described in this chapter, and your dog will be Mr. Manners in no time!

Chapter
eleven

Let Resting Dogs Lie: Training Your Dog to Be Lazy

It's the little, quiet moments that make living with your best friend a successful venture. A dog's playfulness is fun, but by the time most puppies hit adolescence, the non-stop craziness can drive most people absolutely around the bend. By rewarding a dog for lying down, he will start enjoying his rest time. You can train your dog to be lazy and to lounge around the house, ultimately making life easier for you! This is what makes pet ownership a success. It also is what makes living with people successful for the dog—little, quiet moments.

If your dog will settle down for a short while, you can enjoy a lot of quiet time to yourself! You obviously are going to have to make it worth the dog's while to be calm. Reward him for laying down—don't turn it into a punishment. Instead, when your dog lies down, give him a lot of fun chew toys! This

teaches him to require less of your attention, and it makes life with him a more leisurely endeavor for you both.

DING DONG, YOU'RE WRONG!

The first of two common fallacies is that, if you have a small apartment, you should get a little dog rather than a big one. This is so very wrong. Many little dogs are like turbo-charged dynamos that can hit the door, the couch, and the window in about 10 seconds flat, yapping all the time! As a generalization, it is fair to say that it actually is much harder to get little dogs to lie down. Big dogs (such as Newfoundlands, Malamutes, and Rottweilers), however, are wonderful dogs for apartment living. After they walk, they come home and just flop down.

The second fallacy is the notion that you have to give your dog lots of physical exercise if you want him to settle down. People with Pointers and Setters who jog with their dogs are actually training them to build up endurance so that, at some point, no amount of exercise will ever physically exhaust them! You cannot tire a dog out and get him to settle down with just physical exercise unless you let him run all day or you have a breed that has trouble breathing or have a great big lumbering dog. Certainly, dogs need physical exercise and that is part of the fun of having a dog—going out for walks with him and throwing toys for him to catch. If you want a dog to settle down, however, he needs mental exercise. (You have to train him to settle down.) In terms of making a dog livable, this is the key. *Not* taking the doggieness out of the dog, just letting him know that there are times when you need to have some quiet moments—the same way you would teach a child. Let him know that he can be noisy and active when it is appropriate—in the park, at a doggie party, in puppy class, and so on. Also let him know, however, that he eventually needs to settle down. The more you practice this at home and on walks, the better companion dog you will have. Not only will he become a dog that you can turn on and off at the drop of a hat, he will be a dog that is very livable around your home. He won't be bouncing around all the time.

LIE DOWN AND REST A LITTLE, ROVER

When you are at home, call your dog over often and ask him to lie down on the carpet or on the couch. It's great if he chooses to lie in his bed, but you need to be sure you can get him to settle down when and where you ask.

Asking your dog to settle down is great to do when you are reading. After a couple of pages, get up and move to a different chair. Bring the dog with you and ask him to settle. This produces a very livable, low-key dog. This probably is the best on-leash exercise there is. It is great to do with a young puppy or a newly adopted adult dog or any dog that has a whole lot of energy. Put the dog on-leash and step on the leash or tie it to the leg of your armchair. You can help the dog to settle by giving him a chew toy but also do this at times without a chew toy. This develops the dog's desire to want to stay close to you. It also makes it much easier to teach him to

Training your dog to settle down is easy when using on-leash exercises. With a puppy, the leash acts as an umbilical cord, keeping your dog close to you at all times. The puppy will follow your movements and soon will be walking when you walk and sitting when you sit. With active adult dogs, you can tie the leash to the leg of your chair and give him a chew toy. This develops the dog's desire to want to stay close to you.

The Lazy Way

Teaching your dog to settle down is very rewarding:

■ He'll learn to not pull on-leash while taking walks

■ Visitors won't have to worry about being jumped on by an excited dog

■ He will remain calm and well-behaved while home alone

■ He will learn to respect your quiet time, by settling down when you want to settle down

Taking it easy while teaching "Cardigan" to settle down and amuse himself.

come when called and to heel. It may take a few moments for your dog to settle; just ignore everything he does until he lays down, then calmly praise him.

FIRST THINGS FIRST—TEACH HIM TO TAKE IT EASY

The first two things to teach your dog when he comes into your home is to enjoy calmly settling down and to enjoy his own company when you are away from home. Obviously, apart from autoshaping him with chew toys when you are away, the only other way to train a dog to settle down while you are away is to start doing it when you are home. One of the biggest mistakes people make when they first bring a new dog home is they let him run wild. They give him constant attention and let him follow them around the house. Then, of course the dog misses these people when he is away from them. Practice having lots of little, quiet moments when you are home. This really does your dog a favor. He will be much less likely to fall apart when you leave. (It also does you a favor; it gives you a chance to rest up!) Remember, there is a lifetime ahead for activity, rambunctious behavior, and fun and games, if the dog works at it. This basically depends on whether he likes people, is free of behavior problems, and settles down on request—all qualities that can be trained!

Many people miss the golden moments when their dog is settled down. You should go over to the dog, calmly say "What a good dog," and walk away, praising him for being quiet. All too often we focus on our dogs' actions that we don't like, and we never say "Thank you" for the good stuff.

PARTY TRAINING: A QUIET GATHERING

Invite your friends over for a settle-down party. This is a very laid-back dog-training party. All your visiting trainers have to do is see how often and for how long they can get your dog to settle down quietly. Tell them to ignore anything he does other than settling down. When he settles down, the person in front of the dog can calmly praise him and can give him a little piece of dinner

QUICK & PAINLESS

Many people are scared to teach their dog to settle down. Some people ask their dogs to settle down just when the dogs have pretty much relaxed. The real trick to this training, which might seem a bit odd, is to get your dog really jazzed up and then have him settle down. The first time you do this, the dog will not settle down very quickly, but you should still repeat it. Jazz your dog up again and then have him settle down. By the fifth or sixth time you do this, your dog will go from warp factor nine craziness to totally calm. If you think about it, this really makes sense—there's no point in teaching your dog to settle down when he isn't very active. You want your dog to settle down when he is jazzed up.

One great way to teach your dog to settle down is to have him on-leash in your home and to have the leash fastened to your belt. This is called the *umbilical-cord method.* The dog will follow you when you move from room to room. When you sit down in front of the TV or the computer, your dog will learn to settle down within seconds. This also is a marvelous bonding technique and is a way to get your dog to focus on you. Be sure that your dog also continues to spend some quiet moments by himself in his long- or short-term confinement area.

kibble. Your friends will love you for throwing a party like this. It means that, when they come over in the future, your dog will have learned how to be the perfect canine partygoer. He will calmly greet people and will settle down quietly to watch the scene.

ARMCHAIR TRAINING: TURNING A LITTLE HYPER MACHINE INTO A COUCH POTATO

This is a simple, relaxing, and highly effective exercise.

Sit in an armchair with the end of the dog's leash tied to a chair leg. As soon as the dog realizes that you're not going anywhere, he will settle at your side. Read lots of books or watch lots of television and, in just a week, even the most hyperactive of dogs will become an affectionate couch potato over lengthy time periods.

Occasionally, you should move to a different armchair and resettle the dog. Practice how quickly you can settle the dog.

Walking your dog is one of the best ways to speed up settling time. I'm not saying to take the armchair with you (though, if you *really* want to, I can't stop you); there are plenty of places to sit down outside. When most people walk a dog, they walk and walk and walk and the dog gets more and more excited with each step. The dog begins to pull on-leash and attention wanes. Instead of exciting him in this fashion, every 25 yards or so just stop and find somewhere to sit. Read a page from the newspaper or a few pages from a novel. Your dog will begin to settle down quicker with each stop. You can help your dog out by giving him a stuffed chew toy sometimes when you stop.

Dogs learn to settle down very quickly when out for walks. This is because what you are using as a reward for settling down—the continuation of the walk—is one of the best rewards for most every dog.

DOG TRAINS HIMSELF: CALM DOWN

Here again, we have the good old stuffed chew toy as our training aid. You can give this to any crazy adolescent dog or puppy. Set your stopwatch running and watch the dog. Within a minute or two, the dog will be happily lying down minding his own business, busying himself with the chew toy. Pretty simple, huh?

IF YOU'RE SO INCLINED

Invite a few friends over and test your dog's settling down skills. If he begins nudging you and your guests, throw him a stuffed chew toy and watch it work magic. Your dog's attention will be instantly diverted from your gathering.

Just give your dog a chew toy stuffed with some of his dinner and he will train himself to settle down quietly and not to annoy your friends.

Getting Time on Your Side

Time doesn't just pass in minutes and hours—it also feels like it's slipping away when you use it up being aggravated at something like your dog. Expecting him to mellow out awhile just because you ask is unrealistic, and when it doesn't happen you'll get aggravated—what a waste of time! Give your dog a stuffed chew toy and he'll occupy himself while you get on with other things.

Chapter twelve

Doggone! The Fastest Ways to Get Your Dog to Run to You When You Call Him

A young puppy basically has a social bungee cord built in. All you have to do to get him to come is walk away from him and make some noise—click your fingers, whistle, or clap. This works for puppies in a very specific age/time window, specifically 3 months to 4½ months. During this period of time, you can do this exercise outside in a safely enclosed area. You also can do it indoors before the puppy is 3 months old, but remember, you'll have to wait until the pup has his shots to do it outside.

When your pup turns 4½ months old, your time is up! You'll walk away from him, and he probably won't care. If you wait until he has other interests (such as squirrels and other dogs) to instill in him the notion to stay close or to come when

you call, these other distractions will rank much higher than you. So here's a wonderful little exercise you can do with your puppy to make sure you get reliable, happy, willingly compliant recalls in an adult dog.

At dinner time, take a few pieces of the puppy's kibble and walk a little course through your house. Have a competition to see who can get the pup to follow the quickest. If you try this exercise off-leash outside, be sure to do it in a safe, enclosed area.

Whatever the puppy does, you do the opposite. If you've got a very confident puppy that walks ahead of you and walks more than 20 yards away, turn around and run and hide. (Remember, this should only be done in a safe area with no cars around for miles if the area isn't enclosed.) What the puppy learns here is that he is living with a total ding-dong who *he* can't let *his* eyes off of for one second; otherwise, his owner will be lost.

So you hide and watch the puppy. If the puppy gets a little panicked, you can make a little noise or say "Puppy, puppy, puppy." When he finds you, give him pats, praise, and treats—then go off walking again.

Once you do this about three times, there won't be a fourth because the puppy won't take an eye or ear off you. He knows his owner has a tendency to get lost, and this instills in him the notion to stay close.

Recall with a dog like this is an absolute piece of cake. You can use a piece of kibble to train him. When you clap your hands, the puppy comes to you. Get a hold of his collar and give him the piece of kibble. This very conveniently can be done in the living room with the family sitting around, calling the dog from one person to another.

It also is a great way to exercise your puppy or adult dog in the park. Have two people stand about 20 yards apart and call the dog back and forth. (With all the running from one person to another, the dog probably goes 20 miles!) Each time the dog completes the recall, you should pat him, praise him, and maybe even throw a toy for him to fetch or give him some kibble. A piece of cake!

It's not a bad idea to have your pup on a long leash as a backup. If he doesn't come when you call him you can use the leash to give him a little guidance in your direction.

PARTY TRAINING: CALLING ALL DOGS!

This will probably be your dog's favorite training party. At this party, he gets to be the center of attention and to run from person to person. Basically, you are playing round robin with the dog. Each person can call the dog one at a time. When he makes even the slightest movement toward that person, the individual should begin to praise him. When he gets all the way to the person, he or she can use a lure (a toy, a bit of kibble, or a treat) and ask the dog to sit. Be careful, this game can make your dog very happy. Be sure to pause and let the dog spend a moment with the person who just called him before the next person begins.

A COMPLETE WASTE OF TIME

The following are the three worst ways to teach your dog to come when called:

1. Not training the behavior as a puppy.

2. Punishing your puppy (when he eventually gets to you) for slow responses. This is how you train him not to come. Eventually, slow recalls become no recalls.

3. Unintentionally punishing your puppy for coming when called (e.g. calling your dog to end a play session). Instead, call your dog to come and sit many times within the play session. Give him a pat and a piece of kibble and tell him to go play again. When it is time to go home, give your dog three liver treats when he comes when called.

It is just as easy for a dog to do things with style as it is for him to do them clumsily. Instead of just having him come and then taking his collar and giving him a treat, have him come and sit in front of you as it's done in an obedience ring. It's a piece of cake to do. Call the dog and praise the first step he takes toward you. (Don't stand there glumly.) Praise him all the way to you or he might find that squirrel in the bushes to be a more interesting prospect than you. When he is two dog-lengths away from you, hold your hand out with the food treat and say "Rover, sit!" It often helps if you take one step back as you say this. It helps him sit straight since he is doing it in motion.

ARMCHAIR TRAINING: HEY ROVER, COME 'ERE!

This is similar to the party method of teaching your dog to come when called. At times when your family is hanging out and relaxing, call the dog back and forth. Be sure that, whenever he comes to you, you gently get a hold of his collar and then praise him. The reason for this is to ensure that your dog likes to sit when people hold his collar. You don't want a dog that runs to you but then skirts away when you go to hold him.

DOG TRAINS HIMSELF

Work your dog with a trained dog. First, call your dog and then call the trained dog. The first dog to you gets a food treat. You'll find your dog soon teaches himself with a little help from you and a canine buddy, of course, warp factor recalls!

Getting Time on Your Side

As Maria von Trapp proved in *The Sound of Music,* start bringing up people's favorite things and you'll have them paying attention in no time! The same is true for dogs. What are most dogs' favorite things? Treats! Choose your pup's favorite, walk away from him, call him to you and offer the treat, and when he reaches you, reward! It's so quick and easy you'll be singing this method's praises.

Calmly Quieting that Overzealous Barker

Y ou can't punish an animal for being an animal, and it's a plain fact that dogs bark. Punishing a dog when he barks is just as stupid as punishing the dog when he wags his tail. One of the biggest problems most people have is that they try to train their dogs to stop barking forever (the first mistake) and at the worst possible moments (the second mistake). These bad times include when the dog is completely worked up and barking at people at the front door, at a squirrel climbing up a nearby tree, or at another dog that happens to be prowling around the front yard. Needless to say, these are not good times to try to train a dog to control his bark. Instead, train your dog to stop barking when he is calm—this is easier on both you and the doggie.

First teach your dog to bark on command. After this, the "Shush!" command will be a cinch!

Teach your dog to speak on command. This is a wonderful trick; people love it when you can get your dog to reply to questions such as "Do you want your dinner?" You'll also find that, if you have successfully taught your dog to speak on command, you will not have a barking problem—it's as simple as that.

PARTY TRAINING: DOG BARK PARTY

Parties offer a wonderful opportunity to teach your woofer to bark on cue, so invite guests to a dog barking party. Instruct your guests to arrive at different times. Instruct them they should not ring the doorbell until requested. That is, until they hear you say "Speak."

Pay attention to your dog. Urgently say "Speak! Speak!" (the cue for your guest to ring the doorbell). This will stimulate the dog to bark. Praise your dog for barking. (This alone will probably blow his mind and will get him to attend to you a bit.) Then say "Rover, shush!" and waggle a really tasty treat in front of his nose. As soon as your dog sniffs the treat, he will be quiet. Wait two seconds, say "Good shush," and offer the treat.

Have each guest leave and repeat the sequence throughout the visit, increasing the length of the woof and shush periods in each sequence. Dogs just love this exercise. They get to listen to and watch the door, feverishly praying that the doorbell will ring! This exercise makes for an extremely vigilant watchdog. If the dog barks at other times (without the doorbell), tell him go to the kitchen and settle down—a little time out from the party scene. The dog will soon have the speak command down. At future woof parties, you can have your guests play woof relays. Then say "Rover, shush!" Get out a tasty treat and waggle it in front of his nose. As soon as he sniffs the treat, he will be quiet. Wait two seconds, say "Good shush," and give him the treat. Go out again with each guest throughout the evening. The dog will get this down very quickly. Then you can have other people take over the training.

ARMCHAIR TRAINING: DOGGIE TALK

I love having conversations with my dog. (This is convenient because I live with a very verbal dog.) One reason people get dogs in the first place is for companionship and protection. Training him to bark on command offers good protection and, of course, good companionship comes from chatting with him. Dogs can be easily trained to bark, whisper, woof, growl, and make all sorts of weird sounds. Now you can sit in an armchair with your dog at your side and can ask him all sorts of questions. "What do you want to watch on the television? Do you think *Frasier* is funny? Do you want to get on the couch?" Then give him his speak command and a pet or a pat. Dogs love it! I often ask my dog if she wants to come on the couch. It's a "woof, woof!" and then she'll jump up! But, if she woofs before I ask her to she is sent out of the room. She is now very careful to speak only when asked to.

DON'T BE COUNTER-PRODUCTIVE

If you do any of the following when your dog barks, you are just wasting your time *and* your dog's time.

1. **Putting a barking dog outside.** Obviously, the barking will get worse. A dog will hear many more noises outside (from other dogs and from neighbors). His barking will carry much farther there, too.

QUICK **PAINLESS**

Most people, at one time or another, feel like their dog will bark forever—he won't; he'll stop. When he does stop, say "Thank you" and give him a treat. Be sure to praise him three times over—"Good dog, good dog, good dog"—before you give him the treat. This way, you are not rewarding barking when you give him the treat. You are rewarding his quietness. It is quite amazing how quickly this changes the frequency of a dog's barking spells. What most people do, of course, is ignore the dog when he is quiet and give him loads of attention when he is barking. People think they are reprimanding the dog, but the dog really is thinking how great he is because he got his owner to join in!

2. **Putting a dog outside that isn't housetrained or chew-toy trained.** If you do this, your dog will become a barker very quickly. Simply housetrain and chew-toy train him and then he can just stay inside.

3. **Punishing the dog when he is barking by squirting him in the face with all sorts of noxious substances.** This will only teach the dog not to bark when you are around. Other than that, it does nothing. If anything, it exacerbates the whole notion of owner-absent barking.

Getting Time on Your Side

The first way to get time on your side when dealing with an overzealous barker is to work with him when he's calm; otherwise you may provoke rather than teach him. Work on the methods described in this chapter on TV commercial breaks while the mute button's on. Remember, practice makes perfect, even if it's just a minute here or there.

Chapter fourteen

How to Stop a Digging Terror Without Wreaking More Havoc

Digging is another one of those very normal, natural and necessary doggie behaviors. What would you say if someone told you they wanted to teach their dog to never wag his tail? Well, the prospect of teaching a dog never to dig sounds about as ludicrous to me. Dogs dig for all sorts of reasons, not the least of which is for fun. And you certainly don't want to be known as a party pooper. Kids love to dig and we have a simple solution for them, just use the same for your dog. Kids have sandboxes; your dog can have a digging pit.

CANINE TREASURE TROVE

Pick a spot in your yard and let your dog watch you bury a few bones, chew toys, and treats. Then, encourage him to dig by scratching at the dirt and your dog will get the idea. Praise him for digging in the spot. Have a camera ready to photograph your dog's shocked expression. He'll be thinking "After months of being yelled at, now my owner wants me to dig?" If you are careful to supervise the time your dog spends in the yard, you can redirect him to his digging pit if he tries to dig somewhere else.

Digging and barking usually are just the tip of the iceberg—the real problem often is that the dog is not housetrained or chew-toy trained. These problems prompt the dog's relegation to the backyard where he learns to dig and bark.

Another part of the solution is the good old stuffed chew toy routine. Use this to retrain the dog so you can leave him in the house without his causing damage. Using a long-term confinement area will also help.

The dog still may bark a little, but it won't bother the neighbors as much. Digging certainly won't be a problem inside. Many people confine their dog to the outdoors with the rationale "Oh, he likes it out there." But the grim reality often is that this person just didn't house-train the dog. If you ask the owner why the dog was brought into his or her life in the first place, the answer probably is for companionship and protection. But who is the dog keeping company or protecting in the backyard?

Keep your dog in your house. View going into the yard as a communal thing—you go out there together and have fun together.

IF YOU'RE SO INCLINED

You can help your dog to stick to using a very specific area as his digging pit by bordering the area. Decorative stones or wood can make a very pretty and immovable border.

PARTY TRAINING: BRING AND BURY PARTY

Train your dog *before* he spends any time alone in the yard, and teach him where he can dig. By throwing a bring and bury party, your friends can help you train your dog to stop digging up your yard.

In a bring and bury party, everyone brings something to bury in the dog's digging pit! This is a fun thing to do. The dog then can go out to his digging pit and what a bonanza, what a find.

ARMCHAIR TRAINING

You can't do this from your living room, so pull up a lawn chair or swing in your hammock in the fresh air while engaging in this method. Again, digging usually results from an untrained dog being put outside in the yard without supervision. First, train your dog *before* you put him outside. Second, teach him where he can dig—the digging pit. Third, spend time with him in the yard. Read the newspaper out there and keep an eye on him. Watch what he is doing and praise him when he's good. If the dog even thinks of walking on the garden—let alone digging in it—instruct him to go to his digging pit.

DOG TRAINS HIMSELF

Talk about easy . . . just bury a stuffed chew toy in his digging pit!

A COMPLETE WASTE OF TIME

Expending all of your energy trying to prevent your dog from digging is definitely a waste of time. Dogs dig because it is a natural doggy behavior. They dig to bury food, to make dens for puppies, to find warmth in the cold weather and cool earth in the warm weather, and for plain old fun.

Getting Time on Your Side

A digging dog? Problem solved: Don't waste time discouraging him from doing his doggy thing; instead, designate a spot where he can dig to his heart's content and be rewarded for it. It's much more fun for both of you.

fifteen

Supersitter! Sit and Relax . . .

Do people admire your dog from a distance because they don't want his muddy paw marks all over their clothes? Teaching your dog greeting etiquette is a snap, and he will thank you for showing him how to get all those distant admirers to come a little closer.

Of the many dog misbehaviors that have been unintentionally taught by the owners, jumping up is probably the best example. Ever since the dog was a puppy, he has been trained to jump up by the owner patting him on the head and laughing. The dog's only crime is that he eats and grows and continues to jump up. Of all the so-called crimes dogs commit when living with humans, jumping up is the one that prompts some of the most horrendous abuse. People take hold of the dog's forepaws, squeeze the paws, squirt lemon juice and Bitter Apple in his mouth, knee him in the chest, hit him on the head with a rolled-up newspaper, step on his hind toes, and flip him backwards. Why? Because he jumped up— something he was probably trained to do during puppyhood.

When the dog gets older, however, the rules become reversed. Jumping up now is something he is punished for—how confusing!

Not only is punishing the dog for this behavior confusing, ironically, it usually exacerbates the problem. Try to consider the dog's point of view—what does jumping up mean in doggie language? Pawing, jumping up, play bowing, and anything that has to do with bending the elbow says "Hey, I'm trying to be friendly."

So this little dog comes up and says this and what do we do? We clobber him. What does this do? It causes the jumping up to increase in frequency. Why? Because the dog jumps up to apologize. After all, you just punished him.

If your dog has a softer temperament, he may use other doggie behaviors to communicate to you that he is happy to see you and that he is submissive to you. One of these behaviors is quite offensive to people—submissive urination. This problem should be viewed as a red flag. Your dog is not confident in greeting people; in fact, he probably is a bit scared.

Instead of punishing the dog for this behavior, why not just prevent it from happening at all? Train your dog to greet people properly. How about teaching him to sit when greeting people? If you make it rewarding for him to greet people this way, why would he do otherwise?

Think about what your dog finds rewarding—a toy, a ball, maybe a bit of his kibble? How about that all-important commodity—human attention. By teaching him that proper greetings get him one or more of these

Outdated training methods often advocate numerous unpleasant, physically arduous, and time-consuming procedures for stopping dogs from jumping up.

things, you will have a dog that puts his rear on the ground when people approach faster than you can say "Good doggie!"

YOU'LL THANK YOURSELF LATER

If you teach your young puppy to sit when greeting people, you will never have to deal with the problem of jumping up. If he gets praise and an occasional food or toy reward for sitting when people say hello and is ignored when he jumps, he will very quickly realize which option is more rewarding!

QUICK **n** PAINLESS

Reward your dog with "Good dog, Rover!" or give him a treat whenever you see him sitting. This simple reward training very quickly produces a sit-happy dog (a dog that simply spends more of his time sitting). And if he is sitting, he generally is out of mischief.

It is much easier to simply teach the dog how you would like him to greet people.

PARTY TRAINING: SUPERSITTER FIESTA!

Have a supersitter party. Better yet, how about a Super Bowl Sunday supersitter party? Invite a bunch of people over and give each person five pieces of dry kibble. Have a competition to see who can get the dog to sit the most during commercial breaks.

Show each person how to use the lure/reward method—that is, while you hold a bit of food, gently rub your hand against the dog's nose. Slowly raise your hand back over the dog's head. He will follow the lure in your hand and, when his head tilts back, where will his hind end go? To the ground! Think of your dog as a see-saw. If one end goes up, the other end goes down. After a few repetitions of this behavior, your dog will start to get the idea that the only way to get the tasty morsel out of each person's hand is to sit.

For naysayers who are thinking "Well, then I have to use food all the time" or "I want him to do it for me, not for food," let me respond to these often-voiced comments. After about 10 minutes of getting the dog to sit for food and giving it to him each time, you will move on to what is called a *variable ratio of reinforcement schedule*. I know it sounds technical, but it just means you use the treats sort of like a slot machine—you keep him guessing as to when he will get a reward. Think of your dog as a gambler in Vegas. He "plays" you and sometimes gets a "Good dog!" Sometimes you reward him with something a little more special (like a toss of a tennis ball or a treat). And sometimes you give him a jackpot payoff (like an extra special little treat or a little game of chase). I often tell my dog Oliver what a good guy he is. Sometimes, when he does something especially great (like running to me really fast when I call him, as opposed to his usual Gordon Setter lope), I give him a

YOU'LL THANK YOURSELF LATER

Practice quick sits at least 50 times a day. It's simple to do, and it's the ultimate training session. Most people think training sessions are an hour spent at a dog-training class—not so. The best training session is one that is about three seconds long. But you'll need to do at least 50 or 100 of them a day. The best one to practice is sitting. You basically aim to get your dog up to 95 percent reliability. Very few trainers can get a dog beyond this. If you do, however, you'll have a great emergency command. There are a couple thousand behavior problems your dog can't engage in after that.

A sit test was designed by Dr. Ian Dunbar. The dog had to sit eight times. The situations for each sit request changed slightly, and most obedience trial champions failed. After 2,000 dogs tried this test, only two had passed all eight tries. One example from this test is to put your dog in a down stay and lie down in front of him so that you and your dog make a straight line with your head 2 inches away from his front paws. With your hands by your side, calmly say "Rover, sit." Another example is to have someone hold your dog on-leash while you stand about 5 yards away with your back to the dog and say "Rover, sit!" If your dog can do these two, give yourself (and, of course, your dog) a super bonus reward.

jackpot reward of hugs and kisses and lots and lots of verbal praise.

Another way to think of this is you are rewarding your dog similarly to how your place of employment rewards you. Most people do not get paid for each task they accomplish at work, right? The schedule of reinforcement for most people is about every week or two weeks, a *fixed schedule ratio reinforcement schedule*. Your dog can do you one better by working for a *random* schedule ratio of reinforcement.

ARMCHAIR TRAINING: YOU SAY GOOD-BYE, I SAY HELLO

When your dog jumps up, he is only trying to say hello. Don't turn him away, just explain to him how he *should* say hello.

If you want to go for the most relaxing way to train your dog to sit, do it from an armchair. Dogs generally are more inclined to jump up on people who are standing. So call the dog from your armchair and instruct him to sit.

Occasionally, as a big surprise, stand up and invite the dog to jump up for a hug (if you want your dog to be able to jump up on command). Your dog learns that the default setting to greet people and to receive pats and food treats is to sit. Now and then, however, if you are so inclined and are wearing appropriate clothing, you might be open to a hug.

DOG TRAINS HIMSELF: HE'LL LEARN ANYTHING FOR A TREAT

One of the best training techniques is to let the dog work out how to do something all by himself. This allows him to use his brain, and it provides us with the opportunity to see how quickly our canine friends can learn. Let the dog work out how to greet people appropriately. Show the dog that you have some tasty treats in your pocket and then just stand there. Don't interact with your dog at all. Simply ignore all the dog's inappropriate antics. The more excited the dog gets, the more he learns what doesn't work to get your attention or the treat. The dog will eventually sit. When he does, say "Good dog" immediately and offer a treat. Then take one step and repeat the procedure. In just half a dozen or so repetitions, the dog will sit the second you stand still. He will learn that sitting is the best ploy to get treats, and he will start to use this greeting with many people. Try using a stop watch to time how long it takes him to get this concept. I bet it won't take more than five minutes.

The only way to get reliability is through repetition. Let your dog meet lots of friendly people, but be sure to calmly and gently help him choose to sit. For a few weeks, carry around a little toy or a few pieces of his dry food and use them to reward him for sitting. When you meet nice people on the street, ask them to give your dog the reward. (Be sure your dog is friendly with people.) The more frequently your dog sits to greet people, the more likely he will be to continue to do so.

Get a trainer to teach your dog to sit reliably and then have him show you how to do it. It may help you to have a trainer get the dog started with some good training, but you still need to follow through with what the trainer has taught you and the dog.

The Lazy Way

Getting Time on Your Side

Stopping your dog from jumping up on people is even less strenuous than getting time on your side—all it takes is getting other people to use *their* time. You just sit back and watch! Arm your team with pieces of kibble, follow the advice in this chapter, and you're on your way to a sitting-greeting dog.

Chapter sixteen

Lazy Luke Leashwalker

When training a dog to walk nicely on a leash, there are only two rules: Do it in a secret disguise and don't go anywhere! If your dog is not yet trained, it is a good idea *not* to make an idiot of yourself on the street. (Hence the disguise.) This is particularly important for dog trainers walking their untrained dogs (always a considerable embarrassment). Of course, you can always use the excuse that you're training a client's dog, but even this excuse wears a bit thin when you're walking the same dog—your dog—around the same block—your block.

The following puts leash walking into an easy to follow five-step format:

1. **Follow off-leash**: First teach your dog to follow you when off-leash. This should be done inside at first and then in a safe, enclosed area outdoors. Use anything you can think of to motivate your dog to want to stay close to you. This can be a happy tone of voice, a toy, some of the dog's kibble, or just playfully running away from him and encouraging him to chase you.

QUICK ✦ PAINLESS

Try a promise collar, one of several marvelous devices used in the halter system, which gives you a mechanical advantage over your dog. This is very handy if you are a small, weak person and have a very strong dog.

2. **Walk at your side off-leash:** Next teach your dog to walk at your side while off-leash using lure/reward training. Ask him to walk with you for a few steps and then lure him into a sit position and praise him. This is how you teach the dog to sit quickly when you stop and to pay attention to you and follow you when you walk. He will want to stay with you because he likes you and because it is rewarding to do so.

3. **Stand still on-leash:** When your dog sticks with you off-leash, you are ready to put the leash on and do a reward-training routine. Stand still and give a treat and praise your dog when he sits. Then take a step and wait for your dog to sit again. Repeat this several times and your dog will sit immediately when you stand still. Start to increase the number of steps you take between sits. Soon you will have a dog that watches you and stops when you do—you will have a dog that walks nicely on-leash.

4. **Walk on-leash inside:** Set up a walking course in your home from room to room and around tables and chairs. Once your dog trots calmly by your side on a loose leash, it is time to venture to the streets outside.

5. **Go outside on-leash:** But don't go anywhere! I know this sounds silly, but read on.

THIS DOG WAS MADE FOR WALKING, AND THAT'S JUST WHAT HE'LL DO

There are basically just a few reasons for walking a dog:

- for the dog's enjoyment—a good walk and a sniff
- for your enjoyment
- to get from A to B, e.g. from the front door to the car, or from your home to the dog park
- to allow your dog the opportunity to "empty out"

Let's talk about walking a dog just to walk a dog (to find out about walking a dog for him to empty out, check out Chapter 8). The essential ingredients of enjoyable walking are that the dog walks close to your side when requested and sits when you stop and that at other times he may range and sniff without exerting undue tension on the leash. The reasons why many owners experience difficulties walking their dog are twofold: The owner is distracted and/or in a hurry and doesn't pay attention to what the dog is doing such that the dog pulls and gets away with it and also that pulling on-leash is both incredibly and intrinsically reinforcing. If the leash is tight the dog doesn't have to pay attention to you as the leash acts as a sort of telegraph wire for the dog to know where you are. Again, the solution is simple, when training your dog to walk on-leash, don't go anywhere!

For the next few days, walk your dog with the sole intention of training your dog to walk in a civilized

A COMPLETE WASTE OF TIME

Continually jerking your dog to get him to stop pulling is probably the most commonly taught method. The dog pulls; you say "Steady," and then give him a jerk. With a very good trainer, this may work. It obviously doesn't work when most people do it, however, as evidenced by the fact that they still are jerking their dog and the dog is still pulling. This brings up a very important question—when you tried something, did it work? If it didn't, I suggest quickly changing to a different method.

fashion. With a handful of your dog's breakfast or dinner dry kibble in a plastic bag in your pocket and a good book or newspaper in your hand go outside and stand around with your dog on-leash and wait for him to sit. Ignore all the dog's antics. It doesn't matter whether the dog jumps, barks, or pulls on-leash. Ignore all inappropriate behaviors. Strangely enough but utterly fortuitous, the more the dog misbehaves and the more we ignore the bad behavior, the deeper good behavior will be entrenched at a later date. Basically your dog is working out all the ploys that don't work and eventually, the single ploy that does—sitting.

Eventually your dog will sit, if only for a second. The instant the dog sits, say "Good dog," offer a piece of kibble, and then take one giant step and stand still and wait for the dog to sit again. The single step will reactivate the dog. This time though, the dog will likely take less time to sit. Once he does—same as before—good dog/kibble/giant step. After just 10 or so sits, you will find your dog will sit the instant you stand still after each step. Now try taking two steps before stopping for the dog to sit. Then go for three steps in each walk-step sequence. You'll find the dog becomes surprisingly attentive and does not pull on-leash. Instead your dog eagerly anticipates each standstill so he may sit to claim another piece of kibble. Now take 5 steps in each sequence and then 8, 10, 20, and so on. You will now find your dog walks calmly and attentively by your side and sits promptly and eagerly whenever you stop—we call this walking on-leash. And you've trained your dog to do it without a single correction and by only uttering the lovely words "Good dog!"

Now comes the real pay-off—time for the both of you to get the most out of walks. Alternate periods of walking on-leash (signaled by a suitable request to "keep close" or "by my side") with periods when you allow your dog to range and sniff (signaled by a suitable instruction to "go on" or "go sniff"). Be careful not to allow your dog to tighten the leash when ranging. If he does, simply stand still until he comes and sits by your side. This will accustom your dog to sitting close when you stand still in response to the approach of distractions like people and other dogs. Sometimes you can reward this closeness with a treat or by allowing the dog to go ahead and investigate the distraction.

PARTY TRAINING: HEEL-SIT COMPETITIONS

Invite people over for following and heel-sit competitions around a living room course. Let your guests know that no dinner will be served until each person has successfully completed the course with the dog. You also can have a picnic with your puppy or dog and go on a long walk with the pup on a long line. Wherever the puppy goes, you move in the opposite direction. If the puppy lags, you speed up; if the puppy runs ahead, turn around and go backward. Each time you reverse direction the puppy will keep closer and closer to you—you're developing an invisible umbilical bungee cord!

YOU'LL THANK YOURSELF LATER

Never let an untrained person walk an untrained dog. Nothing will teach a dog to pull on-leash quicker than this. One of the most reinforcing actions in all of dogdom is for a dog to be able to put tension on the leash and to take a few steps forward.

Once your dog has become a "chew-toy-aholic" the chew toy can be used as a lure and a reward to teach your dog virtually anything.

Once you have trained your dog using a variety of lures your dog will look to your hands for signals.

IF YOU'RE SO INCLINED

Teaching your dog to pull on-leash can actually be a wonderful thing to do. The dog will look at you like you are daffy when you let him pull you the first time. The first time you ask him to walk by your side again, however, it will be much easier. You basically are alternating the problem of pulling on-leash and the way you want the dog to walk therefore incorporating the problem behavior into the training regimen. By alternating, it is easier for your dog to learn what you want. By putting the problem on cue, it is, of course, no longer a problem. It now is an obedience command that you have trained.

ARMCHAIR TRAINING: TRAINING IN COMFORT

Armchair training is less about sitting in a chair and more about training in comfort. It is difficult to teach a dog to walk on-leash outside because you often feel inhibited with everyone watching. The dog usually is extremely excited because there are so many distractions. Therefore, you should do it in the comfort of your own home. Go around a furniture obstacle course. You even can try going to a place that is temperature controlled (such as a local dog-friendly hotel).

Have a picnic when your puppy is 3 to 4½ months old and go on a long walk with him on a long line. At this age, puppies have a very strong desire to follow their owners, so just keep walking away from him. Whatever the puppy does, you do the opposite. If the puppy lags, you speed up; if the puppy runs ahead, you turn around and go backwards. If he gets more than 15 yards away, you run and hide. You want to panic him a little, to make him think he has really lost you. If he gets more than 25 yards away, let out little "beeps"—"puppy, beep, beep, beep"—so he starts to look for you again. After you have successfully hidden from him a couple times, he will not let his eyes off you again; he will keep close. From now on, when you walk with him and do reverses of direction, he will keep much closer to you—developing this invisible umbilical bungee cord (which in itself pretty much solves the leash-walking problem). Each time you reverse direction, you will find that the puppy keeps closer and closer.

DOG TRAINS HIMSELF: REWARD TRAINING REDUX

Develop a good relationship with your dog by hand feeding, petting, and playing games and he will want to walk close to you. Also, don't fight to get your dog's attention on-leash. Instead, walk away from him and make it his job to stay close to you.

IF YOU'RE SO
INCLINED

If you train your dog to pull on-leash and you live in a hilly area, you've got a winning combination. There is nothing like having a big dog pull you up the street.

Getting Time on Your Side

Forget about fighting your dog all the way down the block while he pulls you along behind him. You gain no time playing that game with him! *The Lazy Way* to address the issue is to make the energy-conserving choice to follow the five-point plan outlined in this chapter. Soon you'll be looking forward to the time you spend walking with your dog.

Chapter

seventeen

Timeless Tricks in No Time!

Believe it or not, there *are* easy, cheap, and fun ways to train your dog to do tricks. Tricks, like anything else, are easy to teach from an armchair (is there a better place from which to ask your dog to fetch the newspaper, the remote control, or your slippers?) or by having a social gathering. And you'll have lots of fun playing around with your dog!

TRICKS ARE FOR KIDS (AND ADULTS, AND PUPS, AND DOGS...)

Why teach tricks? Why not? Teaching tricks certainly is better than the much-too-popular, adversarial, combative approach to dog training in which dogs are pushed, pulled, and jerked around in an attempt to force them to act against their will. At least people crack a smile when teaching tricks, and dogs love learning them. For example, most children can teach a dog to play possum quicker than Mom or Dad can command the dog in a dominance-trained "Down!" Tricks really are no

different from any other obedience command, except you ask the dog nicely. The dog is only too happy to oblige and, when he does, you laugh and giggle and clap your hands.

FACILE FETCHING AND TIMELY "GO-TO"

Two of the best tricks to teach your dog are to fetch and to go to objects. If your dog can do these two things, he can run errands for you. He can fetch your slippers or your remote control. The neat thing about the fetch command is that you can teach the dog to grab all sorts of objects. For each new object you teach him to fetch, you are expanding his vocabulary and teaching him to discriminate between objects. The other bonus with the fetch command is that, once the dog understands that "Fetch keys" means go and look for the keys, pick them up, and bring them back to you, you can tell the dog to fetch your keys when you've lost them! This works brilliantly not only with keys but with something else that always seems to get lost—the remote control. Even though the human eye can't find it, the dog's nose will know exactly where it is!

The best way to teach a dog to fetch is with reward training. Get some of the dog's kibble in a bag. Stand in the kitchen and put any object your dog can comfortably and safely hold in his mouth on the floor. Ignore everything the dog does until he looks at the object. If you are impatient, you can just touch it with your finger. As soon as the dog looks at it, say "Good dog" and give him a treat. Eventually, the dog will start pawing or nosing this object. Say "Good dog" again and give him another treat.

The dog soon learns that finding interest in this object is the key to the food vending machine—you! He will start nosing it, nosing it, nosing it. Eventually, he will pick it up and then it's "Good boy, good boy, good boy . . . you get a treat for that!" The dog will immediately drop the object to get the treat. Wait for the dog to pick the object up again and then praise him. "Good dog! Good dog!" When he drops the object, try to catch it in your hand. By the fifth time you do this, you want to wait until the dog picks up the object and holds it for a couple of seconds. If he drops it instantly, that's okay—just ignore it. The dog will soon go back, pick it up again, and hold it. "Good dog, good dog, good dog, thank you!" With this praise, he'll give it up. You are building a pick-it-up, hold-it, drop-it-in-your-hand routine. The dog really is doing something like picking up a coin and dropping it into a food machine. Pretty soon, the fetch bit becomes easy—the dog knows he can work you for food by dropping a specified object into your hand. Toss the object in front of you, just a couple yards away. The dog will go to pick it up and bring it back. Place the item farther and farther away. You also can have the dog sit while you place the object somewhere outside the room. The dog will have to search for the object to bring it to you. Start with one object and then add another such as a tennis ball, leash, squeaky toy, or whatever else you have around. I'd draw the line at the TV though.

The Lazy Way

QUICK ⬛ PAINLESS

By now you are probably no stranger to the power of doggie treats, so add them to your list of miracles. Soon your dog will fetch and even learn new vocabulary words simply by tempting his tummy with the lure of his favorite kibble.

The second great trick to teach your dog is to go to different places or people. Again, once the dog has the concept that "Go to" means go somewhere or to someone, it can be a great vocabulary-building exercise. Now you have another great vocabulary-building trick to teach!

I like to start with teaching a dog to go to a certain place. The best examples include telling your dog to go to his bed, to go outside, to go inside, or to go to the back seat of the car. These are examples of useful vocabulary. To start with places, have someone hold the dog out of the room. Go place a treat in the dog's bed. Open the door and say to your dog "Go to your bed, go to your bed, go to your bed!" Eventually, he will go to the bed and find the treat. If you do this about half a dozen times, the dog will get it pretty quickly. "Go to your bed" means to go to bed. And that's where there is likely to be a treat.

You can take this one step further. Tell the dog again to go to his bed. He does so quite happily now because, when he has done so on other occasions, he has found treats there. This time, when the dog trots over to the bed, tell him "Down" and then give him the treat. Do this about a dozen times, each time having the dog lie down for a little bit longer. He is learning that "Go to bed" means to go there and lay down for a few seconds, and you will come over and give him a treat.

Try this with the back seat of the car. Lure the dog to the back seat and give him a treat for sitting there. Next time try it, but before you lure him onto the seat say "Rover, get in the car."

"Go outside" also is a good command. It is very important for a dog to be able to differentiate between inside and outside for the purposes of housetraining. If you housetrain your dog in your house, things will go well until it's time to visit someone. (You don't want Rover peeing all over your friend's new rug. The only way to prevent this is to make sure he has learned the concepts of inside and outside.) He may go down to the basement and think, "Hey, this is outside." Stand at the back door if there's a yard or by the front door with a leash. Stand there with some of the dog's dinner kibble. (This is kind of like she loves me, she loves me not.) Say to the dog "Outside," and then throw the kibble outside. The dog will go out to get it. Then say "Rover, inside," and throw the kibble inside. If you do this randomly, calling out "Inside" and "Outside" as appropriate, the dog will learn that when you say "Rover, outside," the kibble goes outside and that the kibble goes inside with "Rover, inside." This is a good thing to do at doorways. The first time I went to dog-training class with my adolescent dog, I told my dog "Inside" and "Outside" to make sure he realized that the classroom was inside and that house rules applied there too (as in no urinating and defecating).

SHAKE, ROLL OVER, LICK YOUR HAND

To teach your dog to roll over, lure him into a down position. See which side his back legs are coming out. Put food on his muzzle towards the side that the two back legs are coming out. Move the food to turn the dog's

YOU'LL THANK YOURSELF LATER

Developing your dog's vocabulary can facilitate housetraining, obedience training, and teaching tricks.

head and the dog will flip on his back, tickle his tummy, and he will roll over.

To teach your dog to kiss you, rub a bit of freeze-dried liver on the back of your hand and tell the dog to kiss you.

To teach your dog to shake, simply hold a piece of food in your hand, say "Shake" and lift one of your dog's paws. Each time you lift it give the dog a bit of food. After a few repetitions your dog will get it that lifting a paw is what gets the treat.

The reason these tricks are so good is because they all mean something in dog language. When a dog licks you or raises a paw, these are ways in the doggie dictionary to say that he is being friendly and appeasing. He is showing respect towards you. It is wonderful to get this on command. If ever you are worried that your dog is thumbing his nose at you or that he is getting a little upset with you (or fearful or aggressive), you can ask him to come, sit, shake hands, lick your hand, or roll over. As the dog does these things, it helps him get back on an even track.

Getting Time on Your Side

Won't your friends and family be impressed when they discover you've taught your dog to fetch, roll over, or play dead? Think this will only happen if you have a lifetime of lesson plans? Think again! The most time-saving part of teaching tricks is in your dog's responsiveness—he's going to love performing for you because it's going to make *you* happy and get *him* treats. Time will fly as the two of you trick train together.

More Lazy Stuff

How to Get Someone Else to Do It

Getting someone else to do it is the essence of lazy dog training. This section includes tips about doggie day care and finding a trainer, just in case your training partles don't go as well as you expected.

FINDING A TRAINER

Ask your veterinarian and other puppy or adult-dog owners for suggestions or references. Alternatively, you can call The Association of Pet Dog Trainers at 1-800-PET-DOGS. Most importantly, though, try to visit a training class beforehand so you can pick up plenty of ideas to work on at home before you attend the class with your puppy or dog. You'll also get a feel for whether you and your dog would enjoy the class. It is so important to remember that your dog's education and your peace of mind depend very much on you making an educated choice when selecting a trainer.

DOGGIE DAY CARE

There are two general types of doggie day care: Either your puppy attends a day-care center or a dog sitter looks after him. He can go to the sitter's home, or the sitter can come to yours. Day care is a valid option to consider during your puppy's first couple months at home.

If You Want to Learn More, Read These

TOP TEN DOG BOOKS

1. *How to Teach a New Dog Old Tricks*. Ian Dunbar. Oakland, CA: James & Kenneth Publishers, 1991.

2. *The Culture Clash*. Jean Donaldson. Oakland, CA: James & Kenneth Publishers, 1996.

3. *Don't Shoot the Dog: The New Art of Teaching and Training*. Karen Pryor. New York: Bantam Books, 1984.

4. *On the Road with Your Pet*. Andrea Arden. New York: Fodor's Travel Publications, Inc., 1998.

5. *How to Raise a Puppy You Can Live With*. Clarice Rutherford and David Neil. Loveland, CO: Alpine Publications, Inc., 1982.

6. *The Perfect Puppy*. Gwen Bailey. New York: The Reader's Digest Association, Inc., 1995.

7. *Owner's Guide to Better Behavior in Dogs*. William Campbell. Loveland, CO: Alpine Publications, Inc., 1989.

8. *Dog Behavior: An Owner's Guide to a Happy, Healthy Pet*. Ian Dunbar. New York: Howell Book House, 1999.

9. Behavior booklets on *Preventing Aggression, Housetraining, Chewing, Digging, Barking, Socialization, Fighting*, and *Fearfulness*. Ian Dunbar and Gwen Bohnenkamp. Oakland, CA: James & Kenneth Publishers, 1985.

10. *An Owner's Guide to a Happy, Healthy Pet*. (A series of books about individual breeds by a variety of authors.) New York: Howell Book House.

Still Begging for More?

TOP TEN DOG VIDEOS

1. *Sirius Puppy Training*. Ian Dunbar. Oakland, CA: James & Kenneth Publishers, 1987.

2. *Training Dogs with Dunbar: Fun Training for You and Your Dog*. Ian Dunbar. Oakland, CA: James & Kenneth Publishers, 1996.

3. *Dog Training for Children*. Ian Dunbar. Oakland, CA: James & Kenneth Publishers, 1996.

4. *Training the Companion Dog*. Ian Dunbar. Set of four videos including the topics: "Socialization," "Behavior Problems," "Leash Walking and Jumping Up," and "Recalls and Stays." Oakland, CA: James & Kenneth Publishers, 1992.

5. *Good Puppy*. Jeanne Carlson. Seattle: Sound Dog Productions, 1988.

6. *How to Raise a Puppy You Can Live With*. Clarice Rutherford and David Neil. Loveland, CO: Alpine Publications, Inc., 1996.

7. *Family Dog*. Richard Wolters. Raleigh, NC: Mid Carolina Media, Inc., 1998.

8. *Take a Bow . . . Wow! Easy Tricks Any Dog Can Do*. Virginia Broitman and Sherri Lippman. Doswell, VA: Take a Bow Wow, 1995.

9. *Bow Wow—Take 2*. Virginia Broitman. Doswell, VA: Take a Bow Wow, 1997.

10. *Dogs, Cats & Kids*. Wayne Hunthausen. Donald Manelli & Associates, Inc., 1996.

Take a Bow Wow videos can be ordered directly from the publisher at 1-800-Bow-Wow-2.

Dr. Ian Dunbar's books and videos may be obtained directly from the publisher:

James & Kenneth Publishers
2140 Shattuck Avenue #2406
Berkeley, CA 94704
(800) 784-5531

D

If You Don't Know What It Means/Does, Look Here

The notion of requiring you, the reader, to browse through 10 to 15 pages of a glossary is a teeny bit antithetical to the purpose of this book. So this glossary is very brief:

Autoshaping   Designing the dog's environment to maximize the likelihood that he will train himself.

Chew toy   An item that is both indestructible and non-consumable. If a chew toy is destroyed, it has to be replaced; consuming a non-food item can put the dog's health at risk. A chew toy is intended exclusively for the dog's chewing activities.

The Lazy Way   The quickest and easiest way to train your dog. *The Lazy Way* is not a cavalier approach to training; it is a thoughtful approach. It is an ongoing quest to make training more enjoyable for both dogs and owners so that both will enter into the training game with boundless enthusiasm and commitment.

Lure/Reward Training   The easiest, most efficient, most effective, and most enjoyable way to train a dog. Training takes little time because the dog is lured to perform the desired behavior. Training is effective and enjoyable because the dog is rewarded for desired behaviors.

Luring   A non-contact way to entice the dog to perform the desired behavior following the appropriate command. Luring adds amazing speed to the training process and makes training seem like magic.

Prompting   A way to induce a response. Generally, there are two types of prompting: physical prompting and non-contact luring. Physical prompting involves gently guiding the dog into the required position following the appropriate command.

Proofing   A way to systematically increase the reliability of the dog's responses by progressively increasing the difficulty of the response and the level of distractions.

Reward   A valued commodity or activity given to the dog following good behavior. The reward reinforces the good behavior, causing it to further increase in frequency.

Socialization   An ongoing process in which the dog develops his preferences and needs for specific social contact. A dog may become socialized towards other dogs and require and enjoy their company, or a dog may become socialized towards humans and similarly require and enjoy our company. Without a doubt, socialization is the single most important part of a puppy-raising agenda. Without sufficient socialization, the dog is not completely domesticated and usually becomes an unsuitable companion.

It's Time for Your Reward

Reward Table

Once You've Done This . . .	Reward Yourself . . .
Prepared your home for your puppy/dog and invested in all the necessary doggie products	Treat yourself to some pampering products of your own. Experiment with new perfume/after-shave scents or try some extra-bubbly bubble bath.
Taught your puppy/dog to tolerate time alone	Take your family to that new block-buster you've all been dying to see.
Housetrained your puppy	Hire a cleaning service to clean your house from top to bottom—the way you always want to do it, but can't find the time.
Chew-toy trained your puppy/dog	Buy yourself a box of imported chocolates (and hide them from the rest of the family).
Taught your puppy/dog to settle down when requested	Settle right down with him—in front of a fire with an oversized pillow and a great book.

Once You've Done This . . .	**Reward Yourself . . .**
Socialized your puppy/dog	Catch up with some old school friends over dinner. Then invite them back to your home for coffee or a nightcap to show off your well-behaved pet.
Taught your puppy/dog when to bark	Go on a day-long family outing and encourage Rover to bark where he can let loose and not bother anyone!
Taught your puppy/dog in to shush	Burn some incense or light some candles in a dark, quiet room and enjoy the sound of silence.
Taught other people to train your puppy/dog	Take advantage of the time you've saved by learning a new hobby. How about learning another language, taking up country line dancing, or joining a walking club?

Where to Find What You're Looking For

Now you can do these tasks, too!
The Lazy Way

Starting to think there are a few more of life's little tasks that you've been putting off? Don't worry—we've got you covered. Take a look at all of *The Lazy Way* books available. Just imagine—you can do almost anything *The Lazy Way!*

Clean Your House The Lazy Way
By Barbara H. Durham
0-02-862649-4

Handle Your Money The Lazy Way
By Sarah Young Fisher and Carol Turkington
0-02-862632-X

Care for Your Home The Lazy Way
By Terry Meany
0-02-862646-X

Cook Your Meals The Lazy Way
By Sharon Bowers
0-02-862644-3

Take Care of Your Car The Lazy Way
By Michael Kennedy and Carol Turkington
0-02-862647-8

Learn Spanish The Lazy Way
By Vivian Isaak and Bogumila Michalewicz
0-02-862650-8

*All Lazy Way books are just $12.95!

additional titles on the back!

Build Your Financial Future The Lazy Way
By Terry Meany
0-02-862648-6

Shed Some Pounds The Lazy Way
By Annette Cain and Becky Cortopassi-Carlson
0-02-862999-X

Organize Your Stuff The Lazy Way
By Toni Ahlgren
0-02-863000-9

Feed Your Kids Right The Lazy Way
By Virginia Van Vynckt
0-02-863001-7

Cut Your Spending The Lazy Way
By Leslie Haggin
0-02-863002-5

Stop Aging The Lazy Way
By Judy Myers, Ph.D.
0-02-862793-8

Get in Shape The Lazy Way
By Annette Cain
0-02-863010-6

Learn French The Lazy Way
By Christophe Desmaison
0-02-863011-4

Learn Italian The Lazy Way
By Gabrielle Euvino
0-02-863014-9

Keep Your Kids Busy The Lazy Way
By Barbara Nielsen and Patrick Wallace
0-02-863013-0

For further information about additional dog training and behavior books and videos by Andrea Arden and Dr. Ian Dunbar please contact:

The Center for Applied Animal Behavior
2140 Shattuck Avenue #2406
Berkeley, CA 94704
(800) 784-5531
www.manhattandogtraining.com
www.siriuspup.com